SAY IT LOUD!

BECOMING YOUR HUSBAND'S PERSONAL CHEERLEADER

ROBYN MCKELVY

SAY IT LOUD!

— Becoming Your Husband's Personal Cheerleader

ISBN: 978-1-939268-198
Printed in the United States of America

www.robynmckelvy.com

Dedication

For Ray,

I will continue to cheer for you all the days of my life.

I love you,

Robyn

CONTENTS

Introduction

Say It Loud!

This book contains thirty devotionals to help you build up your husband through encouragement. Walking through this daily activity will give you the heart of an encourager. As your husband receives this encouragement, it will give him the confidence and support to know he is valued. Knowing you value him will give him the determination he needs to accomplish all that God has set before him to complete.

As women, we are natural encouragers. We have encouraged our children so that they can go to the potty on the "big pot." We have taken the time to teach little ones how to tie their shoes (over and over again) with patience. We have shared stories and read books with great detail and in weird voices to any child who wanted or needed a pick-me-up. Encouraging others is just part of who we are and who we were made to be.

This devotional is based on the slogan from the '60s and '70s: "Say it loud! I'm black and I'm proud!" African-Americans' pride was stripped because of the indecencies of other people and this slogan was a voice of hope. Now we can use this slogan for another purpose — building up our families, regardless of our ethnicity.

Today, we are allowing one of the things we should be proudest of to crumble. Our families are dying and it starts with our lack of building an attitude of hope into the life of the leader of our family. Although he is the leader, he still needs support through the encouraging words from his family, especially his wife.

A corporation consists of a team that works hard for the company, and that hard work says to the leader of the company: "we believe in you." This "good job" attitude is what propels the leader to continue and the company to succeed. Likewise, we need to propel our husbands forward and it begins with us building into his life by what we say and how often we say it.

Each day you will:

1. Read a short devotional
2. Answer a few questions.

3. Read a Bible verse.
4. Complete the "Say It Loud" portion.
5. Then **read out loud** to your husband.
6. And finally, get yourself some encouragement from God's Word.

While it may seem obvious to some, I want to reiterate that you will say the "Say It Loud" section to your husband **out loud**. Every day. If you aren't used to this kind of communication, it may seem awkward at first but it is absolutely necessary to gain the full benefits of not only this devotional, but also the strengthening of your marriage. After just a few days of this exercise, he will look forward to hearing your heartfelt words and you will benefit from his renewed appreciation and an increased closeness in your relationship.

You can become a daily encourager to your family and all of its members. You are the role model and primary teacher of encouragement, both inside and outside your home. This book will give you the tools to not just think what you want to say, but to "Say It Loud!"

CHEERLEADER TIP:

Each cheerleader must try out for the squad. She desires the privilege of being the upfront encourager of her team. She enthusiastically accepts this coveted position.

DAY 1

Thanks for Choosing Me!

~

When your husband asked you to marry him, it was the second most important decision he has ever made. The most important was his decision to live for Christ.

No doubt he took time to think about his future with you and what it would look like. The decision he made when he asked you to marry him meant he could not foresee the rest of his life without you.

When your husband stood at the altar, he understood the choice he was making. You may not have been the first or only woman he dated. You may not even be the first woman he thought about marrying, but you were the choice of choices for him. At the altar, he made his vows to you and knew that his life would be forever changed. He was choosing to alter his life because he found that life without you would not be life for him at all.

Proverbs 31:10, says, "An excellent wife who can find? She is far more precious than jewels." Genuine jewels are rare and worth tons, monetarily, to their holder. Some jewels are precious because of the quality, the cut, and the size. Other jewels are precious because they are heirlooms, passed down from generation to generation. Your husband believed you would be an heirloom for him and his legacy. You were the "quality" woman, the "cut" above others, and the "size" of your heart drew him to you. He wanted you to be his. There were things he saw in you (strengths, personality, laughter, work ethic, and more) that he knew he and his children would need to acquire.

To your husband, you are his rare find. You are the choice he knew was "excellent" for him. Other versions of the Bible use the word *noble*, *virtuous* (which means a woman of strength), *capable*, *wife of worth*, *of noble character*, and *good*. Your husband understood his choice.

Now we need to take time and look at his "popping of the question" from his perspective. Then we can truly understand the choice he made when he chose you.

1. Read Proverbs 31:10-12. Then, write out the details of your first meeting with your husband.

2. Write out the details of your engagement.

3. Name some of the unique characteristics that you feel attracted you to your husband.

4. What are the ways you are good for your husband?

5. When your husband thinks about you, what are the things he would say he has total confidence trusting you with? Give specific examples.

6. Finally, how are you striving to continually bring your husband good and not evil all the days of your life?

Your Prayer:

Heavenly Father,

I thank You that You do all things well. I praise You for giving ____________ *(write your husband's name here)* to me as my husband. Walk with me as I demonstrate Your love to _________ *(write your husband's name here)*. Thank You for putting us together for a lifetime.

In Jesus' name, AMEN.

Say It Loud: 

________________ *(write your husband's name here)*, **I want to thank you for choosing me to be your wife. I want to be the noble, excellent, capable, good, wife of worth to you.**

E.F.T.W. (Encouragement from the Word):

> *"He who finds a wife finds a good thing and obtains favor from the LORD."*
> Proverbs 18:22

A Cheer to Remember:

My team is the best!
The best in all the west!

My team will always beat,
Anyone in the east!

My team rules the court
Better than anyone in the north!

My team runs the south,
Everybody! Hear me shout!

CHEERLEADER TIP:

She knows (is sensitive) to the unique times when her team needs "extra" support. That's when she uses the special cheer that puts wind beneath the wings of her team.

DAY 2

You Are Hot!

~

Have you ever really wanted to buy something that was in scarce supply?

One Christmas, we wanted to buy the up-and-coming video gaming system for our family. My husband and son ran to the store to get one and were informed that the person right before them purchased the last one. The man who took home the coveted item experienced elation and victory. But for us and others who are waiting to receive the next batch — disappointment and anticipation.

Your husband *is* a hot item. Godly husbands are in scarce supply! They're a much-anticipated commodity. There are many women who are looking everywhere to find the gift you have and because of the high demand and limited quantities, your gift is a rare find. Your husband is a man who others would want to snatch up and call their own. But God has graciously awarded this "hot" item to you.

You are God's choice to own and care for this "hot" item — your husband. The care you give him will be reflected by both of you as your marriage is displayed publicly and privately.

Your husband needs to hear from you that you realize he is a much-sought-after commodity and that he is the type of man that is desired by others.

Now that you have received your husband as a precious gift from God, the way you care for him, looking out for his best interests, and building him up with your words will show an on-looking world that he is valued by you.

God has gifted your husband to you. As his only wife, you should show him, daily, that you have obtained favor from the Lord and will receive him as a hot item. He will be able to see this regard for him by how you speak to him, by how you speak *about* him when he is not present, and by how you care for him in even the tiniest of ways. He is your one true hot item and you are the luckiest of women, blessed among others, to have him.

1. What are some things that you know would not be the same if your husband were not in your life?

2. Can you think of an item or two you thought you had to have but never acquired it?

3. Why was having this item(s) so important?

4. Your husband is the thing that you may not have thought you needed but God did. How has God used your husband to change you for His good?

5. Read Titus 2:4-5.

a. How is your marriage honoring to God's Word?

b. What are some ways you display your love to your husband?

6. What are some distinct (unique) qualities that set your husband apart from all other men?

Your Prayer:

Heavenly Father,

Teach me how to be grateful for ____________________. Help me to remember that he has been personally selected by You for me.

In Jesus' name, AMEN.

Say It Loud: 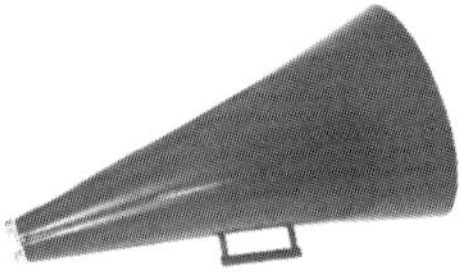

__________________, you are hot and a very hot commodity! You are one of a kind and I am so grateful to call you mine.

E.F.T.W. (Encouragement from the Word):

"My beloved is mine, and I am his…"
Song of Solomon 2:16

A Cheer to Remember:

H-U-S-T-L-E
Hustle team, hustle!

*(Repeat as many times as needed
to make the point!)*

CHEERLEADER TIP:

She understands that certain cheers are appropriate at strategic times. She would never shout a defensive cheer when her team is playing offense.

DAY 3

I Need You

~

Most everyone loves receiving flowers and roses are the most common flower given in relationships. They are beautiful to look at, add a great scent and color to any room, and they represent or remind you of something or someone each time they are given.

I've tried to grow roses at almost every home we have owned but I have found that roses take a lot of work to produce. The flower that we so easily buy to express our deepest sentiments takes much attention and work to yield.

Some flowers are easy to plant, water, and grow. But a rose takes special care. You must first plant and add rose fertilizer, and water and pick off the dead buds, periodically. Then in the fall, you must prune back the branches, cutting the plant away to a fraction of what it used to be. Roses need this care, watering, fertilizing, and pruning to produce healthy, sought-after stems.

We need our husbands, just as they need us. We need them to plant us in fertile soil (void of rocky places). This soil must be mineral filled so it will produce healthy growth. Our homes are like the soil, a place where we should feel safe. Our churches are like the minerals where we find community for healthy growth.

We need our husbands to hydrate us daily, giving us the necessary components for growth. This hydration through his encouragement and conversation is life-giving to us, just as ours should be to him. But, we also need him to be willing to cut away at our branches by bringing to our attention the areas that would keep us from producing the best possible fruit. We need to be willing to hear from our husbands any areas he sees that may not be what is best for us in each season of our lives.

Your life can be a sweet aroma to all you come in contact with. God has given you your husband to aid Him in producing the best "____(your name)_____" you can be.

Ecclesiastes 4:9-12 says, "Two are better than one, because they have a good reward for their toil. For if they fall, one will lift up his fellow. But woe to him who is alone when he falls and has not another to lift him up! Again, if two lie together, they keep warm, but how can one keep warm alone? And though a man might prevail against one who is alone, two will withstand him — a threefold cord is not quickly broken."

You are one part of the two, and your husband is the other part from Ecclesiastes 4:9 above. You should lift your husband up when he falls. You are there to keep him warm when it's cold and you are his ally when the enemy tries to overtake him. Can he say that you are these things to him?

1. What are some of the reasons your husband would say you have aided him to have "a good reward for their toil"? (See Eccl. 4:9.)

____

____

____

____

____

____

____

____

2. Name some positive ways your husband has planted you in fertile soil (your home and your church) where you are growing.

3. How is your encouragement and conversation to your husband hydrating to his life?

4. In what ways can you continue to enhance this encouragement and conversation?

5. What are some areas your husband has suggested you may need to "cut away" for you to produce good fruit? (Family, friends, time at work, etc.)

6. How have you begun to eliminate these suggestions?

7. Read Ephesians 5:22-24.

a. How is your submission to your husband displayed?

b. How is your submission to the Lord displayed?

Your Prayer:

Heavenly Father,

I need You to teach me how to make sure I allow ____________________ to see that I need him. It has become so easy for me to leave ________________ out of so many things I do, and not show him that I need him. I want him to see how much I need him and desire for him to need me. I pray that we never get beyond needing You or each other.

In Jesus' name, AMEN.

Say It Loud: 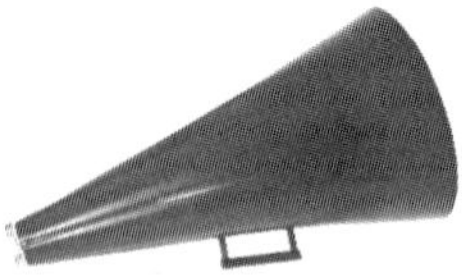

________________, I need you! If I ever fall and need someone to pick me up, I want you to be that someone there to help me. I need you by my side, as long as we both live.

E.F.T.W. (Encouragement from the Word):

> *"Wives, submit to your own husbands, as to the Lord. For the husband is the head of the wife even as Christ is the head of the church, his body, and is himself its Savior. Now as the church submits to Christ, so also wives should submit in everything to their husbands."* Ephesians 5:22-24

A Cheer to Remember:

Let's Go! Let's Go!
L-E-T-S G-O!
Let's Go! Let's Go!
L-E-T-S G-O!

CHEERLEADER TIP:

She is so passionate about her team that those watching her team play the game want to rally behind her.

DAY 4

You're Doing a Wonderful Job

~

I spend a lot of time purchasing things for our home. When I go to the grocery store, I expect that everything on my list will be available. When I'm at the store, it seldom occurs to me to thank the store clerk for having the items available for me to purchase. I am, however, grateful to receive the thanks from the clerk for my business and his or her reminder that they will "see me next time."

Often times our husbands overlook the little things that we do to make our house a home. He forgets to thank us for preparing dinner or tell us that we look or smell nice.

Ever wonder why he forgets these little niceties? It could be because he has forgotten what it is like to receive them. It is difficult to remember to compliment someone when receiving compliments is a distant memory. We have been conditioned to expect a thank you from those we aid but have, on many occasions, forgotten to thank those who aid us.

Remind your husband what it feels like to receive a compliment from someone who knows all his insecurities and inadequacies. He is all yours and a compliment from you will hold more value and weight than a multitude of compliments from any other source. Romans 14:19 says, "So then let us pursue what makes for peace and for mutual upbuilding."

Your husband needs to know he is doing a wonderful job. He is demonstrating a love for God by loving and sacrificing for his family, and having a good work ethic.

If we begin to thank him for the things he does behind the scenes, it reminds him that we do not take him for granted. This same gratitude reminds us not to take God for granted for all He does behind the scenes.

1. List two things you felt were overlooked by your husband (and children) in the last month.

____

____

____

____

2. List two things you may have overlooked that your husband did in the last month.

3. What are some things you do that you believe you should be thanked for doing?

4. What are some things you were blessed with, protected from, or enjoyed that you neglected to thank God for?

____
____
____
____
____
____
____
____

5. Read 1 Timothy 6:17. What does the word "haughty" mean?

____
____
____
____
____
____
____

a. Are there areas in your life where the term haughty may apply to you? If so, list them.

____
____

b. What are the ways where it is evident in your life that your hope is in God and not the uncertainty of riches?

Your Prayer:

Heavenly Father,

I want You to teach me how to build up ____________. Teach me to never take him for granted. Allow me to be the reflection of You in his life.

In Jesus' name, AMEN.

Say It Loud: 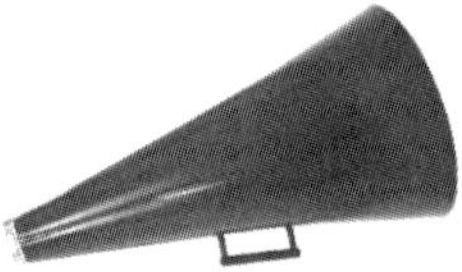

_______________, I want you to know I think you are doing a wonderful job leading our family.

E.F.T.W. (Encouragement from the Word):

> *"As for the rich in this present age, charge them not to be haughty, nor to set their hopes on the uncertainty of riches, but on God, who richly provides us with everything to enjoy. They are to do good, to be rich in good works, to be generous and ready to share, thus storing up treasure for themselves as a good foundation for the future, so that they may take hold of that which is truly life."* 1 Timothy 6:17-19

A Cheer to Remember:

(sing this cheer)

Na, na, na, na, na, na, na, na, na, na, na,
na, na, na, na, na, na, na, na

Go! Fight! Win!

(repeat)

CHEERLEADER TIP:

She understands that she does not cheer alone. She is a part of a squad — encouraging the same team.

DAY 5

I Trust You

~

Trust (noun) 1. reliance on the integrity, strength, ability, surety, etc., of a person or thing; confidence (dictionary.reference.com)

I do trust God. I trust that He created me. I trust that God knows the plans for my life. I trust that God is good and faithful. I trust that He will never change. I trust that though things and times may be hard, God is not capable of failing me nor will He harm me. I trust that God will never leave me and will always be with me.

As I walk with God, trusting every step He leads me to take, I trust that even when the difficult things come my way, His plan is to make me more like Him through it. Therefore, I trust that God has given me my husband. I must trust my husband because not trusting him makes me doubt God. To doubt God means I don't fully trust God.

Trust entails blindly believing you can follow the one you trust, not knowing where He is leading. Can you blindly trust God? If you said yes, then you can trust your husband. Your trust in your husband will not be played out perfectly (we are in a battle and the enemy of God will try to get you to doubt Him) but it should have no reflection on your trust in God. Jeremiah 17:7-8 says, "Blessed is the man who trusts in the Lord, whose trust is the Lord. He is like a tree planted by water, that sends out its roots by the stream, and does not fear when heat comes, for its leaves remain green, and is not anxious in the year of the drought, for it does not cease to bear fruit."

No matter how bad life may be, you can trust your husband because your trust is in the One who gave you your husband. Our trust says we know that God is for us and not against us and He would never do anything to harm us.

1. List the things you trust about God.

____

____

____

2. Think of a difficult time when you had trouble believing God had your best in mind. How did this time grow you in your relationship with God?

3. In Jeremiah 17:7, why is the man blessed whose trust is in the Lord?

4. As you walk in blind trust and obedience to God, how is this demonstrated in your trust of your husband?

5. Read Proverbs 3:5-6.

a. In the Proverbs passage, how are we told to trust in the Lord?

b. What do you believe "with all your heart" means?

c. In your own words, paraphrase the sentence: "do not lean on your own understanding."

d. How has God made your paths straight?

e. How does you trusting your husband show your faith and trust in God?

Your Prayer:

Heavenly Father,

I want You to teach me how to trust __________. Help me not to hold on to what I think is secure, but trust You by trusting my husband.

In Jesus' name, AMEN.

Say It Loud: 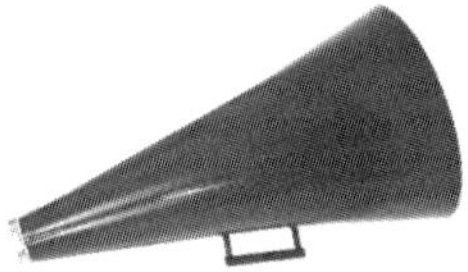

______________, I trust you! I see the beauty of God's creativity by giving you to me to learn to more fully trust Him. Trusting you has shown me that I must not doubt God. I am able to see the wisdom of God by allowing me to walk out life with you. You are a tangible display of God's trustworthiness.

E.F.T.W. (Encouragement from the Word):

> *"Incline your ear, and hear the words of the wise, and apply your heart to my knowledge, for it will be pleasant if you keep them within you, if all of them are ready on your lips. That your trust may be in the Lord, I have made them known to you today, even to you."* Proverbs 22:17-19

A Cheer to Remember:

We got SPIRIT!
Yes, we do!
We got SPIRIT!
How about you?

CHEERLEADER TIP:

She continues to positively encourage her team onto victory…no matter how many "losses" they have endured.

DAY 6

I Believe in You

~

When we were little kids, we all had dreams of what we wanted to be when we grew up. These dreams were often far-reaching and difficult to achieve. We just didn't know any better because as a child, everything seemed possible.

Reality has a way of replacing our dreams with what is achievable. Just as we had our dreams of what we wanted to be, our husbands also had some dreams. Not everything on our dream list (or theirs) was realistic but there are some things that can still be captured or achieved. All we need — and all our husband needs — is some encouragement.

Accomplishing dreams take hard work. As we try to make our dreams reality, we may not get there on the first try and oftentimes, trying to acquire ones' dreams lead to what we would deem as failures. I am sure, Job, who in Job 1:1 is called, "blameless and upright, one who feared God and turned away from evil," never could have anticipated the trials in his life that took everything of value to him. And Dr. Seuss, prolific writer of nearly fifty children's books, tried to publish his first book, *And to Think I Saw It on Mulberry Street*, over twenty-seven times. Both these men, at one time, would have been considered "unsuccessful" if we didn't know the end of their stories.

Your husband has a dream (or two) that he wants to strive for but the reality of a family, a job, responsibility, and all the other demands is keeping him from going after it. You are your husband's "believer." He needs you to believe that although not all of his dreams can become reality, you know there are still several that he can achieve.

Philippians 4:12-13 says, "I know how to be brought low and I know how to abound. In any and every circumstance, I have learned the secret of facing plenty and hunger, abundance and need. I can do all things through Him who strengthens me."

Your husband can accomplish many things through Christ, the source of his strength. He also has been given a tangible gift by God — you — his helper, his believer.

1. What are some of the things your husband wanted to be when he "grew up"?

2. Now as a grown man, what are some of the dreams your husband has now?

3. What is one occasion, in your marriage, where you were discouraged or disappointed, yet experienced a great time of spiritual growth?

4. Read Genesis 2:18 and 2:20.

a. What did God say about Adam being alone and what did He say He would make for him?

b. When Adam had named all the livestock, animals, and birds, he found no helper fit for him. "Fit for him" means "corresponding to him." It means that what was true of Adam in Genesis 2:7 is also true of Eve. What is true of Eve based on Genesis 2:7?

c. When God created Eve, what Adam lacked, Eve supplied. What does your husband lack that you, specifically, supply?

d. What practical ways can you show belief in your husband?

e. Specifically, what are your strengths or weaknesses that would aid in or be detrimental to your husband fulfilling his God-given dream?

Your Prayer:

Heavenly Father,

I want ______________ to know how much I believe in him. Teach me how to be content in plenty and hunger, abundance and need, so he can fulfill each dream You have for him to accomplish.

In Jesus' name, AMEN.

Say It Loud: 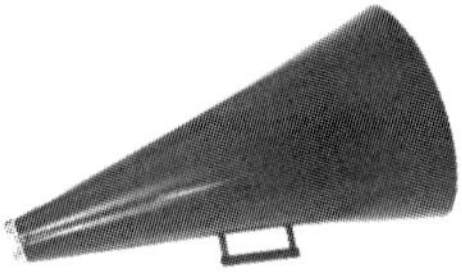

________________, I want to be right next to you as you fulfill the dream God has given you and make it a reality. I believe in you.

E.F.T.W. (Encouragement from the Word):

> *"Let not steadfast love and faithfulness forsake you; bind them around your neck; write them on the tablet of your heart. So you will find favor and good success in the sight of God and man."* Proverbs 3:3-4

A Cheer to Remember:

V-I-C-T-O-R-Y
We will win, I'll tell you why
V-I-C-T-O-R-Y
That's the victory battle cry!

CHEERLEADER TIP:

She would never be caught talking negatively about her team. The cheerleader will remain the die-hard advocate of the team she supports.

DAY 7

I Respect You

~

We show respect every day. We not only must respect certain people because of their positions (police officers, bosses, professors), we must respect inanimate objects as well (crossing or traffic lights, toll-bridges, ATM machines).

For these persons or things, we "respect" and obey them whether we agree with what they are saying or not. We accept a traffic ticket even when we do not believe we ran the red light, and when the ATM machine says our account is empty, we do not get the money, even if we know we just deposited our paycheck.

As a woman who wants to be a follower of Christ, your husband deserves your respect because God commands it (Ephesians 5:33). Your husband deserves your respect because of his position in your home. But your respect of your husband can only be properly displayed if you respect and revere God.

Respecting your husband must never feel demanded; it is a gift. You should freely give this gift because you are offering your respect as a service to God. Once it is freely offered, you cannot decide that your husband no longer deserves it. You must offer your respect to your husband continually, never quitting or disregarding him because you don't feel like his attitude or actions are worthy of respect.

Try not respecting a police officer because he has done something or said something that you don't particularly think deserves your respect. This can land you in big trouble. Ephesians 5:33 reminds us, "However, let each one of you love his wife as himself, and let the wife see that she respects her husband."

Each time you "show respect" to an inanimate object, let it be a reminder that showing respect for your husband is pleasing to God. God is glorified by you respecting your husband. This honoring of your husband is a testimony of your desire to please and obey God's commands.

1. List one person and one inanimate object you personally have to show respect to each and every day.

2. What are the specific actions you show the person or thing above to illustrate your respect?

3. Read 1 Peter 2:18-3:2.

a. In 1 Peter 2:18, God tells servants to obey their masters. Not only the good and gentle ones, but even the unjust. Why is it necessary for us to do this according to 1 Peter 2:19-20?

b. In 1 Peter 2:22-24, with Christ being our example, how did He respond to the ones who made Him suffer?

c. In 1 Peter 3:1, why does the Bible tell us to be subject to our own husbands?

Your Prayer:

Heavenly Father,

I need You to teach me how to respect __________________. As an act of obedience to You, I want to offer my respect to him no matter how he receives it. Show me how to offer unconditional respect to him.

In Jesus' name, AMEN.

Say It Loud: 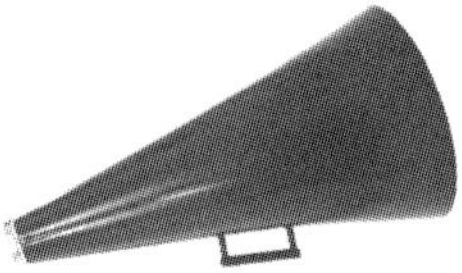

_______________, I respect you. I will continue to offer my respect to you not only as an act of service to God, but also to honor you.

E.F.T.W. (Encouragement from the Word):

> *"Likewise, wives, be subject to your own husbands, so that even if some do not obey the word, they may be won without a word by the conduct of their wives, when they see your respectful and pure conduct."*
> 1 Peter 3:1-2

A Cheer to Remember:

So we will fight, fight, fight for our dear team,
A team we all revere.
And we will fight, fight, fight forevermore.
And give a rousing, RAH! RAH! RAH!
We yell! We yell!
For our team's fame, we'll spread the name of
OUR GREAT TEAM!

CHEERLEADER TIP:

She will only use demeaning cheers
for her team's enemies and foes!

DAY 8

You Are Handsome

~

What makes a man handsome? Most of us would list "looks" in the top three or four qualities of what we find attractive. But what if the most amazingly physical specimen of male is married to your best friend and he treats her poorly? Every lady on the block thinks your friend is so lucky to have such a good-looking man. But you know the secrets. His only good quality is his looks. He is mean to her, belittles her, and abuses her. He is not handsome at all to you, despite his looks.

Handsome, many times, is the description of how a person looks on the outside. But to be truly handsome, it has so much more to do with how you look on the inside.

It is time for us to begin looking at our husbands with God's perspective of beauty in mind. God tells us in 1 Samuel 16:7, "But the Lord said to Samuel, 'Do not look on his appearance or on the height of his stature, because I have rejected him. For the Lord sees not as man sees: man looks on the outward appearance, but the Lord looks on the heart.'" God's definition of beauty begins by first looking at the heart.

A man we would normally consider to be unattractive is still extremely handsome if the Spirit of God is shining through him. But, if the Spirit has no control, even a man blessed with "good looks" is not handsome at all.

Now let's take a good long look at our husbands through the looking glass of the cross. Your husband is the most handsome man in the world if his heart belongs to Christ. Remember, handsome is not solely what you look like on the outside, though that is what the world would describe as such. Being handsome is all about *Whose* you are on the inside; the opposite of the world's definition.

When you begin to look at your husband's beauty by looking at his heart, it will awaken a new appreciation for him in you. God is very creative and He has beauty hidden everywhere. And sometimes it takes us a little bit longer to notice the hidden beauty in familiar things or in people we see every day. Your husband is the same man you have been married to, every day, since your wedding day. Take the time to once again see his internal beauty.

Remember what Song of Solomon 5:16 says: "His mouth is most sweet, and he is altogether desirable. This is my beloved and this is my friend, O daughters of Jerusalem."

1. According to the world's standards, who are the most attractive men in the public eye today?

____
____
____
____
____
____

2. Name five physical attributes that attracted you to your husband.

____
____
____
____
____
____
____

3. Read Proverbs 31:30.

a. What are the two adjectives used to describe charm and beauty?

b. In this verse, who is said to be praised?

c. What does the phrase "fears the Lord" mean?

4. What are five things you admire about your husband's heart?

5. Write a "heart" description of your husband, describing his heart as you would his looks.

Your Prayer:

Heavenly Father,

I need to see ______________ through Your eyes. Teach me, in all things, that handsome is what's on the inside more than what is on the outside.

In Jesus' name, AMEN.

Say It Loud: 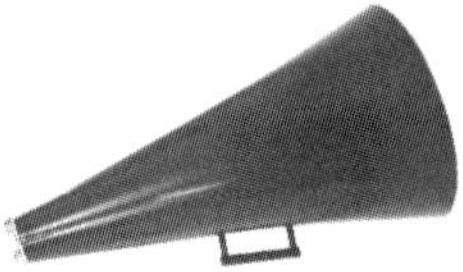

______________, you are a handsome man and you look good to me! I love who you are and would never change one thing about you.

E.F.T.W. (Encouragement from the Word):

> *"O Lord, what is man that you regard him,*
> *or the son of man that you think of him?"*
> Psalm 144:3

A Cheer to Remember:

(Use only for opposing teams.)

U-G-L-Y
You ain't got no alibi.
You're ugly — yes, you are ugly!

CHEERLEADER TIP:

She cares for the team she travels with. She understands her team will need encouragement while they are away from home.

DAY 9

I Will Take Care of You

~

Caring for children is an extraordinary task. It is not for the weak or spineless. It is not for the faint-hearted or fearful. Your responsibility is to care for them in such a way that they mature and grow well. Our care of our children gives them the foundation they need, day in and day out, though it may seem mundane. It may, at times, seem unimportant and trivial. But all that you do is setting them up to be strong, healthy men and women. We should desire to raise adult men and women who are capable of raising the next mature, healthy generation.

Our care for our husband is also vitally important. We have the exclusive opportunity to build into the life of one man, continuing to witness his growth and maturity. We get the privilege of walking alongside him every day. We get to care for him physically as we care for his physical needs; spiritually as we share his experiences in Christ; emotionally as we deal with him — not allowing him to stuff it away; and sexually, being available to share with him erotic love. We care for our husband so he can mature and be all that God would have him be.

If you care for your husband in a godly way, it will spur him on to become closer in his personal walk with God. When we can daily see a picture of God played out in our everyday lives, it causes us to want to look more like Christ, too.

Caring for your husband means taking the good things and the bad things that come up in your marriage. The good things, times where there is little change or conflict, make you feel like your marriage is in a good place. The bad things — times of strife, unexpected tragedy, or difficulties, if responded to properly, make your marriage stronger.

Galatians 6:2-3 says, "Bear one another's burdens, and so fulfill the law of Christ. For if anyone thinks he is something, when he is nothing, he deceives himself."

Your husband needs a true partner in marriage. You are his partner. In being his partner, you are his private burden bearer. Your care for him must begin with continual prayer for any and all things that concern him or your marriage.

Just as we care for our children, we must care for our husbands. When caring for our children, we remove things that may harm them. We pray for their day, the things that they are learning, and the people who are spiteful to them. In the same way, we should, daily, care for our husbands.

1. List the ways you show your care for your children. (If not a parent, think about children of those you work with, family members, and friends).

____

____

____

____

____

____

____

____

2. List the ways your husband would say he sees you caring for him.

____

____

____

3. What are some of the emotional, physical, psychological, or spiritual issues you are seeking to overcome or have worked through in your life or your husband's life?

4. What are some ways you are physically, spiritually, emotionally, and sexually caring for your husband so he continues to mature in Christ?

5. Read Galatians 6:1-10. What are your husband's burdens? In what ways are you bearing them?

6. Are you growing weary in caring for your husband? Why? (Answer even if your answer is "no.")

Your Prayer:

Heavenly Father,

I thank You that You do all things well. I praise You for giving _______________ to me as my husband. Teach me how to care for him and to bear his burdens. Thank You for putting us together for a lifetime.

In Jesus' name, AMEN.

Say It Loud:

_______________, I want you to know I will take care of you. I also want you to know that I want to bear your burdens and care for you for a lifetime.

E.F.T.W. (Encouragement from the Word):

"And let us not grow weary of doing good, for in due season we will reap, if we do not give up. So then, as we have opportunity, let us do good to everyone, and especially to those who are of the household of faith."
Galatians 6:9-10

A Cheer to Remember:

We have come from afar,
To let you know who we are.
We're the WINNERS —
Yes, we're the WINNERS!

CHEERLEADER TIP:

She encourages her team on and off the field!

DAY 10

You Are a Good Provider

~

More often than not, our needs to sustain our lives are normally met. There are times when we may need to ask family, friends, our church, or the government for assistance to get us over a financially difficult time. Most of us have a home with running water and most of us are not malnourished; too many of us are "over" nourished.

With new gadgets coming out every day, it is easy to get caught up in seeing our wants more than our needs. We live in a country where comparisons are all around us. Grades, in elementary school, lend us to comparing. Sometimes things, positions, and wealth cause us to strive to want as much or more than those around us. Children are taught verbally and non-verbally to gain more knowledge than the generation before them, own more possessions, and acquire more riches.

Seeing what our neighbors have can have a tendency to make us note what we do not have instead of looking around our own home to see how much we already have.

God has provided us with so much more than we actually need. To our shame, we sometimes fail to see His provision. In God we have peace, unconditional love, eternal life, and we can never acquire more of these things than we have right now.

Look at your husband. What has God provided you with in him that you have failed to really take note of? I have security, companionship, a warm body to sleep next to, and a love with him that I would have never had without him. To see the intangible things that God has provided in our husbands is to see God's provision. These things alone are the reasons our husbands are good providers. It has nothing to do with what we have or do not have. What we have or do not have is God's provision. God provides what is good for us.

Our husbands have been and will always be good providers — if we stop comparing and see what God has provided in them.

1. Think of a time when you had a need and needed help getting it.

2. Make a list of times when you compared yourself or your circumstances to others.

3. Make another list of all the things that you have that are necessary to sustain life.

**Stop now and take time to pray and thank God for all His provisions.*

4. Take this time and think about your husband. What are some things you see in him that are provisions from God?

5. Read 1 Timothy 6:17-21. What does it mean to "not be haughty; nor to set their hopes on the uncertainty of riches"?

6. What are some of the good things you are doing so that you are "storing up treasure for yourself as a good foundation for the future"?

7. List some ways where your husband has been a good provision for you.

Your Prayer:

Heavenly Father,

I want always to weigh my riches on Your scale. Help me to remember that and know that Your measurements are totally different from the world around me. Allow me to always let _________ know that I see he is a good provider through You.

In Jesus' name, AMEN.

Say It Loud: 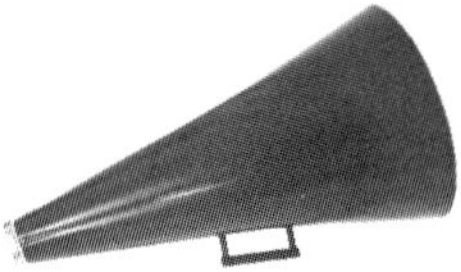

________________, you are a good provider. I am grateful to God for you and the richness of our lives.

E.F.T.W. (Encouragement from the Word):

> *"And my God will supply every need of yours according to his riches in glory in Christ Jesus."* Philippians 4:19

A Cheer to Remember:

Whether we're inside or outside,

(clap, clap)

Our team is the best!
Whether we're uptown or downtown,
Our team passes every test!

(clap, clap)

We will win! We will win! We will win!
I'll say it again!
We will win! We will win! We will win!
I'll say it again!

CHEERLEADER TIP:

She understands that cheerleading won't last forever. She leaves her last game knowing she has cheered for her team to the best of her ability.

DAY 11

You Are a Great Kisser

~

Kisses are all around us. We see kissing on TV, on billboards, at the movies, and any other place where someone feels the urge to display public affection. There are many different types of kisses and they mean a lot of different things. When a baby is born, a gentle kiss from a new mom says, "I love you," as she sees this new creation for the first time. When a child has an injury, a kiss from daddy or mommy to the hurt spot makes it all better. A peck on the cheek of one dear friend to another grieving friend says, "I'm here when you need me," and a long, passionate kiss of a deployed spouse at the airport says, "I can't wait until you return."

A kiss oftentimes replaces words but is exactly the right unsaid act every time you give or receive one. But just as kisses are unspoken words, often romantic and full of life, kisses can also be deceptive. Jesus was betrayed by the fraudulent kiss of Judas. It is so important that our kisses with our spouses are never given with false intentions but out of pure motivation.

I am finding that after years of marriage, my tendency is to kiss out of habit. I kiss but forget to take the time to remember all that used to be said with the meshing of our lips.

Remember back to your dating days with your husband? Can you remember your first kiss with him? Maybe you wondered what took him so long or maybe you wanted another one immediately. The sensation of this first kiss left a smile on your face and you wanted to tell the whole world.

It is time for us to remind our husbands that we want to go back — back to the days that when we leave the house, our kiss means more than "see you later." It is time for us to remind him that our kiss means "I am desperately looking forward to your return to me today." Song of Solomon 1:2 says, "Let him kiss me with the kisses of his mouth! For your love is better than wine…"

What is your favorite drink? Is the kiss between you and your husband better than the sweet trickle of the first taste of this beverage? Your kiss to him and his to you is your display of love and should be so much better than any concoction created. Your love, to him, is "better than wine."

1. Write down two occasions this week where you have seen someone kissing and why they were kissing.

2. Write down the last kiss you gave and your personal reason (your unspoken words) for giving it.

3. What was the occasion for you receiving your last unsolicited kiss?

____
____
____
____
____
____
____

4. Why do you think this kiss was given to you (what were the unspoken words behind this kiss)?

____
____
____
____
____
____
____

5. Do you think that the kisses in your marriage are becoming habitual? If so, why? If not, why not?

____
____
____
____

6. Write down the first time you and your husband shared a kiss.

7. On your next kiss with your husband, what words would you like this kiss to say and what will you be reminding him of?

8. Can you think of a time when you were either given a kiss or gave one and you didn't want to? __________ Recount that occasion.

____
____
____
____
____
____
____
____
____

9. Read Matthew 26:47-50. Judas greeted Jesus by calling him "rabbi" which means teacher. He then betrayed him with a kiss. What are some of the things your kisses are teaching to those who are watching you display this affection?

____
____
____
____
____
____
____
____

10. Knowing that there is always someone watching, how would you change the way you give or receive your kiss?

Your Prayer:

Heavenly Father,

Thank You for creating kisses. Teach me, Lord, to kiss ________________ and never take his kisses for granted. Help me to remember in every kiss I am expressing words with my lips. May my lips always be honest and pure.

In Jesus' name, AMEN.

Say It Loud: 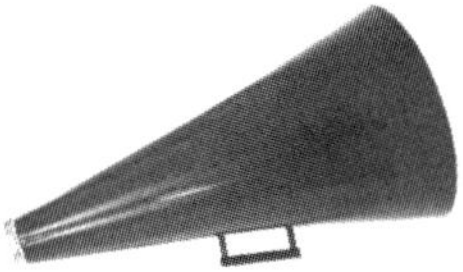

________________, you are a great kisser! I want to remind you, every time I kiss you, that I am so blessed God has given me you to kiss for a lifetime!

E.F.T.W. (Encouragement from the Word):

> *"Whoever gives an honest answer kisses the lips."* Proverbs 24:26

A Cheer to Remember:

Nah, nah, nah, nah,
Nah, nah, nah, nah,
Hey, hey, goodbye!

Nah, nah, nah, nah,
Nah, nah, nah, nah,
Hey, hey, goodbye!

(Your final cheer!)

CHEERLEADER TIP:

She knows the players on her team will have personal failures, successes, ups and downs, yet they play their positions each time there is a game scheduled.

DAY 12

I Love Making Love with You

~

In our culture, most young adults are not given a godly view of sex prior to obtaining education or experience from the world or peers around them. Sex is given so freely, many are often rendered callus by not understanding the repercussions casual sex leaves on our hearts. Sexual intimacy has lost its specialness and has become ordinary. We don't have to look very far to find that sex and the abuse of sex has touched the life of a friend, family member, or even us.

God created intimacy to be exciting and pure. He never intended it to become routine, abusive, or unpleasant. He never wanted intimacy to grow cold and become stale or dreaded. God created sexual intimacy to be shared by a man and his wife for a lifetime of passion.

Our husbands need us to keep a fresh approach to intimacy. We need this approach ourselves. He desires for us to respond to and initiate sex with him.

Our schedules, our children, our jobs, and our agendas keep us tired and overwhelmed. Because we see all these things as necessary, our busyness keeps us unavailable and our intimacy with our husbands is not a priority. We need to respond to him in a new way and throw out the stale, old, mundane, dreaded view of our sexual intimacy. Intimate relationship demands attention so that it doesn't become stagnant. Anything you have that you want to keep in top shape for your lifetime will need to be maintained and protected.

In many of our bedrooms, it is time for a new, lively, anticipated attitude toward our sexual relationship with our spouses. How is this done with the same old spouse in the same old bed? It takes a continued adjustment of right thoughts toward sex.

God created sexual intimacy to allow two people to be closer than any other way possible. This closeness should draw us to a more intimate relationship and loyal friendship with our husband. It is time for us to see intimacy the way God does — being close to your husband in a way that you can never be closer to another. This intimacy with your husband is a picture of your future intimacy with God Himself. There will be no marriage in Heaven and your marriage and the intimacy here shows the love of our Heavenly Father with His bride, the church, to a seeking world.

It is time for those of us who are married to take the time to recommit ourselves to having a fulfilling marriage and a vibrant sexual relationship with our spouses.

1. Can you remember the first time you heard about sex? Write the details down.

2. What was your perception of sexual intimacy after your initial introduction to hearing about it?

3. In your sphere of friendships or family, do you personally know someone who has experienced the devastation of sexual abuse? (yes or no) ______

4. If you honestly looked at your sexual intimacy with your husband, would you say that you spend much time investing in ways to keep it exciting? (yes or no) _____

5. What are some of the things you need to either remove or maintain to allocate time to your sexual relationship with your husband?

____

____

____

____

____

____

____

6. Read Romans 12:1-2.

a. What does presenting your body as a sacrifice mean?

____

____

____

____

b. In verse 12:2, what do you think God is saying by telling us to be transformed by the “renewing of your mind”?

____

____

____

____

____

____

c. What, specifically, does the personal renewal of your mind, regarding your sexual relationship with your husband, look like? (I will need to weed out…, I will need to prioritize my sex life with my husband by…, etc.)

____

____

____

____

____

____

Your Prayer:

Heavenly Father,

I need a fresh attitude toward sexual intimacy with _____________. Renew my mind in this area. Make me experience a new, supernatural approach to having sex that only You can produce.

In Jesus' name, AMEN.

Say It Loud: 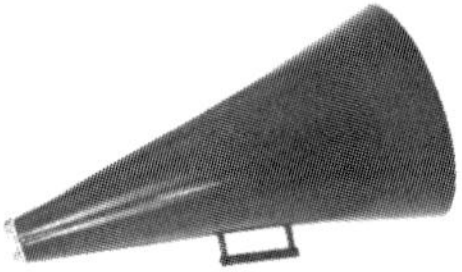

_______________, I love making love with you! I want our intimacy to be a small reflection of our love relationship with Christ.

E.F.T.W. (Encouragement from the Word):

> *"Let us rejoice and exult and give him glory, because the wedding celebration of the Lamb has come, and his bride has made herself ready."* Revelations 19:7

A Cheer to Remember:

We are here for you — say —
we are here for you!

(repeat)

CHEERLEADER TIP:

She understands that life must be lived with humor. Cheerleaders always add fun and humor to each routine.

DAY 13

You Are Fun to Be With

~

While our children are growing up, they have a tendency to remember two extremes: the most unpleasant times and the memorable fun times. Most often, if you ask them to recall a certain family outing, they remember the unpleasant times of that particular occasion a lot faster than the many pleasant memories of that day.

As adults, our memories have a tendency to do the same thing. We focus and put so much energy into the tough times that we have temporarily squelched out the daily occurrences of fun times.

When we first began dating our husbands, almost every date was filled with a lot of fun times and great memories. If the times had not been so much fun, we would have never considered saying "yes" to his proposal of marriage. Too many unpleasant times, prior to marriage, would have made you run from this lifetime commitment.

It is time for us to remember. What made you laugh when you were dating your husband? Can you remember times where you just went out to only have fun and play?

Proverbs 15:15 says, "All the days of the afflicted are evil, but the cheerful heart has a continual feast."

It is time for us to remember the fun times. Times where we laughed so hard with our husbands that it made our sides hurt. Times where the two of you had such a hearty laugh that people looking on could not tell if you were laughing or crying. We must continue to laugh with our husbands. We must continue to make sure we have times of just plain fun and dates where we just play — in the midst of all the stuff we have to do to be responsible.

1. Can you remember the first fun date you had with your husband? Where did you go and what did you do?

____

____

____

____

____

2. Recall the reason of your first deep "belly laugh" you shared with your husband.

3. What are some of the things you and your husband do to just have fun? If none, what would you like to do with your husband to have fun?

4. Read Proverbs 17:22. In your own words, rewrite the verse with what you think it means.

5. Read Proverbs 15:30. In your own words, rewrite the verse with what you think it means.

6. Read Proverbs 15:15 again. In your own words, rewrite the verse with what you think it means.

7. After reading and rewriting the above verses, God is calling us to remember that cheerfulness is needed to help your memories. How will you begin to add cheerful, merry things to your life?

Your Prayer:

Heavenly Father,

Life has squelched out a lot of the fun for ______________ and I. Help me remember the laughter of old and how to make new memories of fun.

In Jesus' name, AMEN.

Say It Loud: 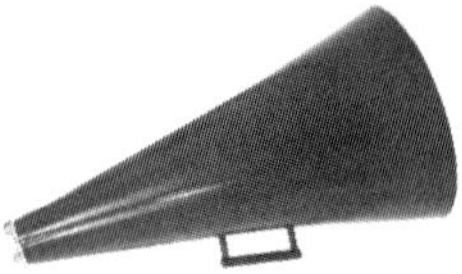

________________, you are fun to be with! I want to create more times where we make memories filled with laughing together.

E.F.T.W. (Encouragement from the Word):

> *"A cheerful heart is good medicine, but a crushed spirit dries up the bones."* Proverbs 17:22

A Cheer to Remember:

We're here to make you laugh;
And then we'll make you cry.
Cause we will win this game and then
we'll say GOODBYE!

CHEERLEADER TIP:

She always has an audience and knows that future cheerleaders are watching her every move. How she cheers will make a lasting impression.

DAY 14

You Are a Great Daddy

~

When Jesus was teaching His disciples on the practice of prayer, He first tells these men that their Father, who sees in secret, will reward them (Matt. 6:4). He then tells them not to be like those who do not know the Father, but that their Father knows what they need before they would even ask (Matt. 6:8).

It is hard to see God, sometimes, as our Father. There are times when you pray to Him and He seems so irresponsive. There are times when we want and need to hear Him speak to us. Times when feel incapable of walking through our situations but we want Him to just tell us what to do. There are times when we don't want to pray and wait on an answer. We want to know now! But God is our Father and He knows the times when He seems most silent are the times we grow the most in Him.

Children need a mommy and a daddy. They need to see a clear picture of what both look like from two uniquely, different individuals. It would be so easy to continue to just do everything for our children as we did when they were babies. But if we continued to allow our children to grow physically and not allow them to grow in their independence of us, we create for ourselves dependent children.

Children who are dependent are usually dependent on the one that they believe will not fail them. And if you have been the provider for all your children's needs, you teach them that *you* are their source and their dependence will be on you. Ultimately, you have taught your children to look to an imperfect provider that will someday die and leave them struggling in their own growth and welfare.

I see times when Ray is silent with our kids. There are times when he just lets them work it out on their own and these are often times I want him to just tell them what to do. But as I silently let him father our children, I see them growing up to be capable, godly young adults. Ray has taught our children, by sometimes being silent, that there is One who is more capable, more dependable, and more equipped to handle their every need. It is their Heavenly Father who is with them as they grow up in our home. He will not leave them when they choose a career path and He will answer all their questions and prayers for the rest of their lives.

As I watch Ray be the great daddy that he is to our children, it reminds me that he is mentoring our children. As he mentors them, his silence is his encouragement to seek their wisdom from above. And that their Heavenly Father will know exactly what they need before they ask.

1. Write out a simple prayer to your Heavenly Father and ask Him for the wisdom you need to wait on His direction and care.

____

____

____

____

____

____

____

2. In your prayer above, what are the things that you sought to ask for wisdom from your Heavenly Father?

____

3. What is one thing you have encouraged your husband to seek wisdom from the Heavenly Father on in the last week?

4. As your husband parents your children, what are some things that he has allowed the kids to walk through with their personal Heavenly Father (i.e., learning to walk as a toddler, sounding out a hard word while reading, letting them drive at night for the first time, etc.)?

5. Is there an outcome to this prayer or how have you seen your kids becoming dependent on our Heavenly Father?

6. Read Matthew 6:5-8. Write out a specific prayer for your husband as he seeks the wisdom of his Heavenly Father to become the daddy your children needs him to be. (If no children, ask for wisdom for your husband as he influences those around him).

Your Prayer:

Heavenly Father,

Teach me how to allow ___________ to be the imperfect daddy our children desperately need. I thank You for Your creativity and that by giving me a husband and father; our children will see a completely unique and different way of parenting.

In Jesus' name, AMEN.

Say It Loud:

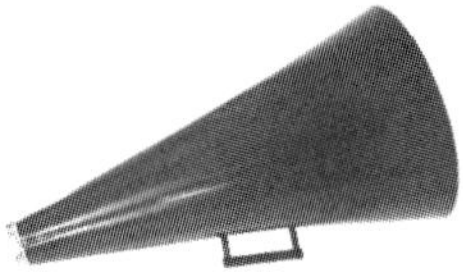

______________, you are a great father! I am grateful your style is different than mine. I will continue to allow you the freedom to parent differently than me so our children will learn to depend on God.

E.F.T.W. (Encouragement from the Word):

> *"Fathers, do not provoke your children to anger, but raise them up in the discipline and instruction of the Lord."* Ephesians 6:4 (NET)

A Cheer to Remember:

We're so proud of you.
I say, we're so proud of you!

(repeat)

CHEERLEADER TIP:

She understands that her teammates must be her friends and any misunderstandings must be positively worked out. Cheerleaders cannot cheer in hostile "home" environments.

DAY 15

You Are My Friend

~

There are many movies, television shows, soap-operas, and homes where it sometimes feels like you are truly "sleeping with the enemy." But we must understand the desperate need to identify who the real enemy is. There is an enemy of your marriage. A being that would love to destroy your friendship and companionship. The enemy is someone who has set out to purposefully do you harm and no good. So it should comfort us to know that we cannot sleep with the enemy because our battle is never against flesh and blood (Eph. 6:12).

Genuine, authentic friendship is a rare find. To be a friend to someone, both must be willing to sacrifice for the best interest of the relationship. To be a friend, you must be unselfish, loving, and trustworthy.

The Bible sets out standards of friendship and it is a high calling. Better is a friend that is near than a brother far away (Prov. 27:10); Faithful are the wounds of a friend; but the kisses of an enemy are deceitful (Prov. 27:6); Like cold water to a thirsty soul, so is good news from a far country (Prov. 25:25); A man of many companions may come to ruin, but there is a friend who sticks closer than a brother (Prov. 18:24); Iron sharpens iron, and one man sharpens another (Prov. 27:17).

When a friendship is genuine, it must be unconditional. This is a friend you can trust at all times. You know your friend will be there to help you when you need help. A friend is available to talk to you when you need someone to listen. Friends understand that to enhance the friendship, it takes time and availability.

Our husband should be one of our closest friends. You should value your relationship with him. Friends care about the things that the other friend cares about. So, is your husband your friend? The only way to know if your husband is your good friend is by judging the quality of your friendship to him.

1. Think of the last movie, soap-opera, TV show, or family where you can recall a married couple who did

not trust each other sharing the same bed. Write the name and the reason for the distrust.

2. Think of a time when you had an unresolved issue with a dear friend and write how you came to resolve that issue.

3. Have you had an unresolved issue with your husband? How are you resolving, or have already resolved that issue?

4. What are some ways where the enemy of marriage has tried to cause discord between you and your husband. How are you battling or how have you battled these issues to bring glory to God and maintain your intimacy?

5. Specifically, name something you have done in the recent past for your husband without "self" in mind.

6. Reread Proverbs 27:10. Why is your husband better off with you close by than having a far-away brother?

7. Reread Proverbs 27:6. What are some wounds you have caused your husband that shows your faithfulness to him?

8. Reread Proverbs 25:25. Write your husband a short letter that would be refreshing for him to receive.

9. Reread Proverbs 27:17. How has having you in his life made your husband become wiser (sharper)?

10. If someone were looking at your friendship to your husband, what would be the positive attributes they would write of you regarding this special relationship?

Your Prayer:

Heavenly Father,

As ________________ looks on our friendship, may it bring a smile to his face. Teach me to be a better friend to him, illustrating the friend You are to both of us.

In Jesus' name, AMEN.

Say It Loud: 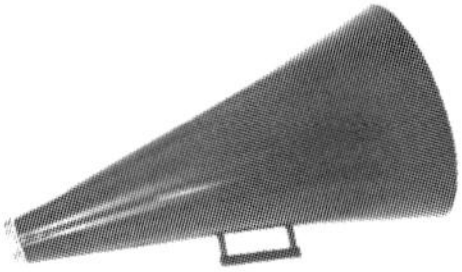

________________, you are my friend! To the end of my days, I will never call you my enemy.

E.F.T.W. (Encouragement from the Word):

"A friend loves at all times, and a brother is born for adversity." Proverbs 17:17

A Cheer to Remember:

Talk it over, Big Team!
Talk it over, hey, hey!

(repeat)

CHEERLEADER TIP:

She understands that every player on the field or court has a specific job to do and will cheer them on as they play their unique position.

DAY 16

I Like Who You Are

~

As children, when others seemed different to us than what we considered normal, we had two extreme responses to them: 1) we would admire them or 2) we would tease them.

As teenagers, those to whom we felt deserved our admiration, we viewed their different quality as something we wanted to attain for ourselves and we would often idolize and deem them important. Ignorance in adolescence causes us to tease anyone whose personality or physical difference is unusual or invaluable *to us*.

Our response to differences as kids should begin to change as we mature into adults. *Kids will be kids* is often the thought of an adult trying to excuse the immature starry eyes or embarrassing laughter of their children's response to someone else's difference.

As we mature into adults, we need to often ask ourselves if we are still judging those in our lives as we did when we were kids, based out of selfish apathy and of our own opinion of what is normal or important.

Proverbs 28:28 says, "When the wicked rise, people hide themselves, but when they perish, the righteous increase." If we do not receive our mate's differences, they may become a shadow of all that God may want to use them to be because they are forced to hide or play down their uniqueness. We all have a need to belong and be accepted for who we are.

God is very creative. The creativity of our Father in Heaven is seen daily in our foods, flowers, and the measure of our faith. As we look at our husband we need to take note of our differences. Everyone who lives in our home should be safe to be who they are and totally accepted. The outside world may want them to conform but our home should be a place where each person should be free to be him or herself, whether they look like anyone else on the planet.

Are you allowing your husband the freedom to be unguarded in your home? He is different from you in every way. God created him just for you and his differences compliment your own unique personality and physical difference. Your husband needs to hear from you that you like who he is — just as he is.

1. Think back to your childhood and name a person you admired and why.

____

____

____

____

____

2. Think of a person you made fun of or teased either publicly or privately and list why.

____

____

____

____

____

3. Do you remember a time when someone was being teased by others and something inside you made you mad?

____

____

____

____

4. List 5 differences you see in your husband, compared to you.

____

____

____

____

____

5. How does God use these differences to complete you?

____

____

____

____

____

6. Read Proverbs 11:12. Rewrite this scripture making it personal regarding your discretion of your husband's differences.

____

____

____

____

____

____

____

7. As you think about the differences you and your husband have, write a prayer thanking God for His creativity.

Your Prayer:

Heavenly Father,

Teach me acceptance. Allow me to accept ____________________ for who You created him to be. Grab hold of my thoughts, actions, and tongue so I will never be the reason he is not free to be himself.

In Jesus' name, AMEN.

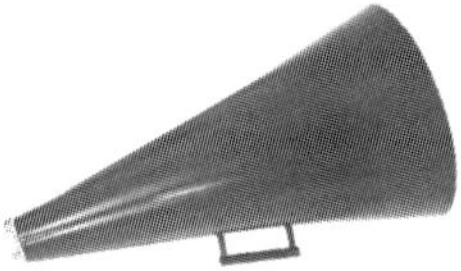

Say It Loud:

_______________, you are unique and I am proud to call you my husband. I like who you are.

E.F.T.W. (Encouragement from the Word):

> *"When I was a child, I spoke like a child, I thought like a child, I reasoned like a child. When I became a man, I gave up childish ways."* 1 Corinthians 13:11

A Cheer to Remember:

You've got to want it!
To win it!
So, do it!
Do it!
Do it!

CHEERLEADER TIP:

She knows that the team will not play every game perfectly. There will be some errors and mistakes, yet she cheers, tirelessly, when these times arise.

DAY 17

You Are a Great Husband

~

Looking at the title of today's devotional and choosing the word "great," not "perfect," is intentional.

What makes a movie great? It must have drama, action, adventure, highs, lows, and love. Doesn't this sound eerily similar to your relationship with your husband? A great marriage will have every adjective listed above, and you share this marriage with one other — your husband.

I have never seen a perfect movie. There is always at least one thing I would have removed or added. I have also never seen a perfect marriage. But seeing the great marriages of those who have gone before me made me want one.

Great marriages are not free of struggle. Great marriages are not made of two conflict-free, complacent people. Great marriages are made in the midst of drama, action, adventure, highs, lows, and love. These marriages have to learn in the midst of these adjectives to forgive, overlook, love in spite of, lift up, build up, and sometimes just shut up. A great marriage is made by keeping the best interests of your spouse as your personal priority.

A great husband is in a marriage where his wife has made it her number one priority to be to him what God has purposed for her to be — his helper. As his helper, you have so much more to offer your husband than just picking up his dirty socks. He needs someone who will follow him as he follows Christ, yet, be the one who will speak the truth, no matter how difficult, in love to him.

Ephesians 5:31 says, "Therefore a man shall leave his father and mother and hold fast to his wife, and the two shall become one flesh." Our husbands stood at the altar, before a judge, or whatever you did on your wedding day to say, "I take you." You said the same thing. Neither of you are perfect and will never be. But he should always be what the dictionary defines *great* to be: highly significant, wonderful, first-rate, and very good.

P.S. A great husband is always the companion of a great wife.

1. What was the occasion of the last card you gave your husband? Can you remember what the card said?

____

____

____

____

2. What is your personal definition of the word "great"?

____

____

____

____

3. What was the last "great" movie (book, TV show, play, etc.) you saw or read and what are the adjectives you would use to describe why it was great to you?

____

____

____

____

4. Which of the above adjectives would you use in describing your marriage relationship with your husband? Why?

____

____

5. What is the one thing you would change about your marriage? (Choosing "spouse," "husband," or the proper name of the one you are married to, are unacceptable answers here.)

6. Read Philippians 2:3. In regards to your own husband, how would you rewrite this verse?

7. What are some unique ways you can personally begin to catapult your husband to becoming or continuing to be great? (Some of these must be areas where you "speak the truth in love" no matter how difficult.)

8. What is the date of your wedding? ____________

a. List some great things about your wedding day.

b. List the great things about your husband on that day.

9. Spend time praying for your husband and then write out a prayer you would pray for him to our Heavenly Father.

Your Prayer:

Heavenly Father,

Thank You for giving me such a great husband in ________________. Help me continue to encourage him to be the greatest husband he can be. Show me how to build him up, how to forgive him when I feel wronged by him, to love him in spite of what I may think is a shortcoming of his, and to know when to be quiet and let You speak to him.

In Jesus' name, AMEN.

Say It Loud: 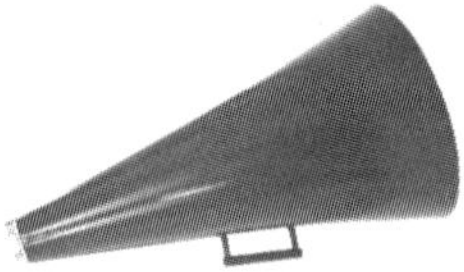

________________, you are a great husband! Thank you for marrying me on ________ (say your wedding date). I look forward to many more great years with you!

E.F.T.W. (Encouragement from the Word):

> *"Therefore encourage one another and build one another up, just as you are doing."* 1 Thessalonians 5:11

A Cheer to Remember:

That's alright! That's okay!
We're gonna win it anyway!
That's alright! That's okay!
We're gonna win it anyway!

CHEERLEADER TIP:

There are certain cheers that must be reserved for special use. These cheers will not be used at every game, but will have a lasting effect at the times when they are chanted.

DAY 18

You Are Special

~

I use the word "special" in two distinctly different ways. There are times when someone who is just plain weird or comedic enters a room and I think, "He's a little special." Then there have been times when I have heard a child play an instrument phenomenally well and I think "special!"

We tend to use the word "special" in extreme yet opposite ways. For example, special coupled with *delivery* is exciting. Special paired with *needs* can seem hard. Really, special before any other word just means something or someone is different than what we consider normal.

Each of our husbands is special and different than all others. That difference is for our good. God created our husband especially for us and for our good. He is different from the norm because he is uniquely yours, made to fit you perfectly by God.

A special item must never be treated as common. It must be treated with extraordinary care that fits its unique purpose. It must be maintained in such a way that anyone who looks on it would see how treasured it is to its owner. To have a special item and to neglect or abuse it strips the uniqueness from it and makes it ordinary.

When you want to celebrate a momentous occasion for a special person, you would choose a fancy restaurant and not a popular fast-food chain. Once at this exquisite establishment, you would expect choice steak and not greasy ground beef. But in order for the restaurant to have the prime cut of steak that would please the finest of palates, it chooses a steak that is raised in particular environments with select care.

Likewise, your husband must be cared for in your home where he is considered the choicest of choices. He must be seasoned throughout the years of your marriage with tender hands desiring him to be a *cut* above.

1. Think of a special time or event in your life and write the event and the details that made it stand out.

____

2. Write your husband a special note, state all the things that make him unique, and send it by mail.

3. In what ways do you see how God has specifically chosen your husband especially for you?

4. List some ways where you can see you have begun to treat your husband as common or ordinary. What can you do to change these ways?

5. When is the last time you had a special event for your husband? What were the occasion and the details of this outing?

6. 1 Corinthians 7:34b says, "But the married woman is anxious about worldly things, how to please her husband." What are some of your marital and family obligations that differ from your single friends?

7. How are you balancing your response to question number 6 with your relationship with the Lord?

Your Prayer:

Heavenly Father,

I know __________________ is special. Give me Your eyes to see how unique he is to You. Teach me how to show him Your favor and place him in high esteem.

In Jesus' name, AMEN.

Say It Loud: 

________________, you are special! I know God made you especially for me, and I appreciate, you, His special gift to me.

E.F.T.W. (Encouragement from the Word):

> *"I praise you, for I am fearfully and wonderfully made. Wonderful are your works; my soul knows it very well."* Psalms 139:14

A Cheer to Remember:

(Repeat this simple children's song instead of a cheer.)

Jesus loves the little children.
All the children of the world.
Red, Brown, Yellow, Black, and White.
They're all precious in His sight.
Jesus loves the little children of the world.

CHEERLEADER TIP:

She always looks for ways to improve her cheers!

DAY 19

I Cherish You

~

Cherish means to admire, adore, care for, appreciate, cleave to, and fancy. There are certain things in my home that I cherish, and I desire to pass them on to my children. I make sure that no intentional harm will be done to these cherished items. The things I cherish, I don't leave out unprotected, and they are only used for special events so that they are not easily broken. Things are made to help us but it is more important to cherish people more than things.

To be cherished by your husband doesn't mean he will be at your beck and call. To be cherished by him is to know he will be there and allow no intentional harm to come to you.

His way of protecting you may only be through his provision of a home that protects you from the outside elements. He may cherish you by keeping those people or things that would try to harm you, physically, spiritually or emotionally, on the outside. He also cherishes you by calling out the things that may be on your inside that may cause harm to you. How are you cherishing him?

To cherish your husband, you must make sure there is nothing, inside or out, that would cause harm to him. Two other synonyms of cherish is embrace and encourage. In cherishing our husband, we must often embrace him. Our touch will allow him to feel our internal warmth and love we have for him, externally. Our continued encouragement to him through our words and actions will let him know that he has a wife who believes in and is willing to follow him.

There are some cherished things in my home that I have displayed for those who enter my home to see. I use this as an opportunity to talk about the things that are important to me. I have pictures of my children at different ages all around and often tell visitors what they are doing and how they are doing. I have multiple pictures of me and my husband around to be able to talk about marriage and my husband in a positive way. I also use these pictures as a reminder for me to pray for my family, their individual struggles, plans, and successes.

As you pray for your husband, God will give you an opportunity to see just how many things are out there that would have a tendency to bring destruction to him. As you pray for him frequently, God uses your prayers to deflect the harm. This is your way of covering him and protecting him.

Cherish your husband like fine china. Treat him with gentle hands, and with a firm grasp through prayer, so nothing will slip by you that would cause him harm.

1. What are the things you cherish? (People and objects are both acceptable answers.)

____

____

____

____

____

____

____

2. Why do you cherish them?

____

____

____

____

3. What are some special things you do or prohibit to care for the things you cherish?

4. What are some of the things that may cause harm to your husband?

5. How is your cherishing of your husband displayed for an on-looking world to see?

6. Read Psalm 83:1-3. In verse 3, it shows how Satan is opposing God and "laying crafty plans against God's people." Your prayers for your husband need to be just as spirited as those of Asaph (the writer of Psalms 83). Write your prayer to your Heavenly Father requesting protection for your husband.

Your Prayer:

Heavenly Father,

Teach me what cherishing __________ looks like. May my regard for him look exactly like Your cherishing of me. Give me wisdom to know the destructive things that are trying to destroy his being a light for You.

In Jesus' name, AMEN.

Say It Loud: 

_______________, I will always cherish you! With God's help, I will make sure no intentional harm comes to you.

E.F.T.W. (Encouragement from the Word):

> *"In the same way husbands ought to love their wives as their own bodies. He who loves his wife loves himself. For no one has ever hated his own body but he feeds it and takes care of it, just as Christ also does the church...."* Ephesians 5:28-29

A Cheer to Remember:

Stomp...
(stomp one foot)

And shake it...
(twist your body from left to right, then clap)

Victory...
(put your arms up into a V, then clap)

Let's take it...
(put your hands down to your right hip and pretend you're taking something then clap).

(repeat 3 times)

CHEERLEADER TIP:

She understands the need to protect her voice when projecting it. She needs to be heard when her team needs encouragement.

DAY 20

I Will Be Your Personal Cheerleader

~

I have seen numerous television shows, movies, and commercials where on the shoulder of a character sits an angel and a devil image of themselves. The devil image whispers bad advice, sways the logic to get the character in trouble, or tells the person he or she is not cut out to accomplish the thing they most want to do. The angel character gives wise advice, encourages the character to go out and do what is right, and spurs them on to accomplish great things.

Everyone needs a voice that is a constant encourager to them; a personal private cheerleader. There are teams that have never won a game, but if they have someone who is willing to praise them just for suiting up and playing the game, it breathes life to them.

Cheerleaders don't cheer at games because they are guaranteed a win. A cheerleader cheers because her team is *in the game*.

Your husband needs a wife who will cheer him on just because he is in the game. As his cheerleader, you are on the field with him, boosting him when he thinks he cannot go on.

When I was a cheerleader, we just didn't have the best of teams. Money was low in our school district and we didn't have the support or foundation that made us an A-1 team. But week after week, our players suited up and played the game. There were times when they played so hard and would lose by a few points. There were other times when you could tell they were beaten before they hit the field. But there were the occasional victories, some even that were said to be impossible.

As cheerleaders, before we went out on the field, we never knew which games would be the victorious ones so we cheered with all our might — every game. If we were down by many points, we felt it was up to us to incite our boys to fight to win.

Our husbands need us to be their private cheerleaders who will cheer them on, with all our might — each and every day they enter the game. Their jobs will reward them for their success they bring to the company. Others will value them based on what they have to offer them. He needs a cheerleader to inspire him through his successes and failures, worth or misfortunes. He needs to be able to hear your cheering voice over his shoulder whispering in his ear, "go, fight, win."

1. What are some ways you are needed to encourage your husband?

____
____
____
____
____
____
____
____

2. Think of a time when you wanted to discourage your husband and made the choice to build him up, instead? What were the circumstances and why did you change your response to him?

____
____
____
____

3. Read Proverbs 14:1. How are you building into the leader of your family?

4. What are some ways you may be tearing him down?

5. Read 1 Corinthians 10:23 (NIV). "Everything is permissible" — but not everything is beneficial.

"Everything is permissible" — but not everything is constructive. How does this apply to your words when speaking to your husband?

Your Prayer:

Heavenly Father,

I want to be a personal encourager for ______________. We all need someone in our corner who cheers us on no matter how difficult situations seem. Teach me to cheer and not tear down.

In Jesus' name, AMEN.

Say It Loud: 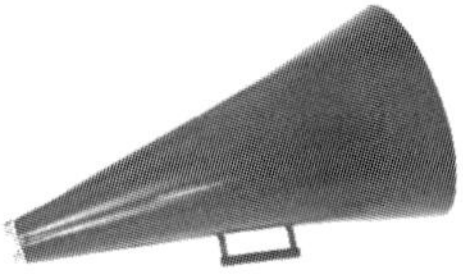

_______________, I will be your personal cheerleader! My cheers for you will be the loudest and most encouraging because in the end, I know we win the game.

E.F.T.W. (Encouragement from the Word):

> *"Let no corrupting talk come out of your mouths, but only such as is good for building up, as fits the occasion, that it may give peach to those who hear."* Ephesians 4:29

A Cheer to Remember:

Rise up to victory,
Our team won't take defeat.
(slap, clap)
V-I-C-T-O-R-Y
(your team name) won't be beat!

CHEERLEADER TIP:

A cheerleader will proudly wear her team colors (pompoms, ribbons, etc.), every opportunity she has to make her team known.

DAY 21

I Want to Hold You

~

"To have and to hold, from this day forward." Most of us repeated this phrase after a clergyman or justice of the peace on our wedding day. What does it mean "to have"? Was this a slick way the clergy was telling me that my husband was mine to keep for a lifetime? What did he mean by "to hold"? Was the justice trying to tell me I needed to hold on tight to him so he wouldn't get away or did it just mean to hold his hand? Whatever is ours to have, we want it to last. We care for it well. Anything we hold, we stabilize or secure.

After delivering each of my children, the doctor immediately gave our child to Ray or me to hold. As we held on tight to the newborn, we brought each of them tight to our breasts to secure them. Our holding of this baby brings security to him or her and it symbolizes our plan to make sure they will always feel secure with us. We need to reestablish holding the one person who God has given us "to have and to hold." In your husband's arms, there is security and stability.

We live in a busy world and some things in life have gotten shoved aside as being less important. We do not realize the urgency of just taking time to hold each other. Holding your husband is a necessity. It is not only a necessary component for him, but also for you. When we take time and just hold each other, we bring stabilization and security to our marriage.

Our relationship with our husband absolutely needs continual stabilization. We are spending far too much money on marriage counselors when we can begin to sure up our marital relationship with a simple act — holding each other. The pastor knows this when he asks us to repeat our vows after him.

I marvel when I think of the security a child feels when he falls down and gets wounded. Each child will begin to look for their own mother to hold them, no other mother will do. Your arms around your baby makes it all better, your arms represent comfort to your child. In the same way, when the wounds of life begin bearing down on your husband, the security he will feel wrapped up in your arms will make it all better.

1. Write down the name of your clergy, justice, or ceremony officiate who performed your wedding and the vows he used to represent "having and holding," (or your own vows if you wrote your own).

2. If you have delivered or adopted a child (or were present for your first niece or nephew, etc.), write down the first moment you were able to hold him/her and your feelings at that moment.

3. What are some of the things you are saving for? Why are these things important to you? How will they bring security to your future?

4. What are some of the things that you have let get in the way of holding your husband?

5. Read Psalm 119:116-117. Rewrite these verses with using your own words.

6. How will the above verses change how you prioritize the things that are important in your life?

Your Prayer:

Heavenly Father,

My busy life has caused me to not prioritize necessary things. Allow ________ and me to learn to hold each other again. In Your way and time, begin to use this time of us holding each other to bring security and stability to our marriage.

In Jesus' name, AMEN.

Say It Loud: 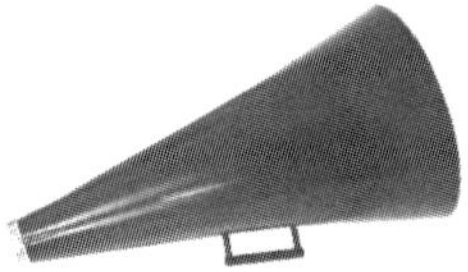

________________, I want to hold you! I want to build lifelong security and stability with you and I know we can begin this by holding each other often.

E.F.T.W. (Encouragement from the Word):

> *"His left hand is under my head, and his right hand embraces me!"* Song of Solomon 8:3

A Cheer to Remember:

Let's *(clap)* get *(clap)* a little bit *(clap on "bit")*
rowdy *(clap on "dy")*
Let's *(clap)* get *(clap)* a little bit *(clap on "bit")*
rowdy *(clap on "dy")*

CHEERLEADER TIP:

Cheerleading is a physical activity that requires strength, agility, and training. It takes a lot of practice and repetition to produce polished routines.

DAY 22

I Love You

~

Recently, I was watching an award show. When one artist won an award, he appeared on stage, accepted the award, and then began blowing kisses and telling his fans how he loved them, over and over.

"I love you" is the phrase we use to express to someone the relationship we have is more than ordinary and they are super special to us. Unfortunately, we have so overexploited these words that they are now just an expression. So, how do you express your love for your husband? Saying, "I love you" is not enough. Love is an action.

If a stranger walks up to you on the street and expresses his love for you, you would think he had mental issues and you would remove yourself from his presence in a speedy manner. Love is more than words;

love is an action and it requires that we act in a tangible way. When you or your husband said, "I love you," for the first time, there had been an investment made between the two of you. You had invested time, conversation, a listening ear, and so much more. How do you show love to your husband now?

In 1 Corinthians 13, the Bible gives us a clear description of what love actually looks like. The beauty of this love displayed in your relationship will never fail. It says love begins by being patient and kind to him. Your display of love to him will not boast about what you've done for him. True love is not arrogant or rude and is not selfish. Your love to him will not be irritated or resentful.

The Bible also says many other things about love — we are to be honest by "speaking the truth, in love" (Ephesians 4:15). God also tells us in Rev. 3:19 that "Those whom I love, I reprove and discipline, so be zealous and repent." These verses show us that love is often hard and uneasy because love is always honest.

These displays of love to him will keep you busy the rest of your life. When you do say that simple phrase, "I love you," your husband's thought should be, "I am truly loved by my wife."

1. Think of a time in the last week where you have heard the words "I love you" and it was no more than an expression. Explain:

___

___

___

___

___

2. Has anyone ever said, "I love you" to you and you really had no history with them? Elaborate:

___

___

___

___

3. When was the first time you or your husband said, "I love you"? What was the setting or occasion?

___

___

___

___

4. Read John 13:34-35. After Jesus told Judas to go do what he had to do, Judas went up from the table to betray Jesus. Then Jesus says these verses to the other

disciples. In what ways is your love for Christ being displayed by how you love your husband to those who are witnessing your relationship?

5. Read 1 Corinthians 13 and give 3 examples of the way you demonstrate this kind of love to your husband.

Your Prayer:

Heavenly Father,

I love _________________ . But in order to display the love You have laid out in Your Word, I will need Your help, strength, and to depend on You. Allow me to love __________ because You first loved me!

In Jesus' name, AMEN.

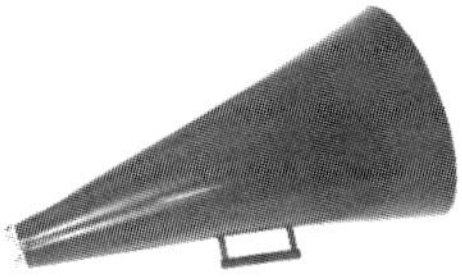

Say It Loud:

____________________, I love you! I pray my display of love to you is felt by you and you will continue to feel my love until death parts us.

E.F.T.W. (Encouragement from the Word):

> *"Love bears all things, believes all things, hopes all things, endures all things. Love never ends."* 1 Corinthians 13:7-8

A Cheer to Remember:

Hustle!
Get to it!
Come on and hustle!
Let's do it!

CHEERLEADER TIP:

A popular cheerleader quote is: "Some wish for it! We work for it!" Cheerleading takes hard work and major effort. A cheerleader never gives up.

DAY 23

Can I Pray for You?

~

When Isaac took Rebekah as his wife in Genesis 25:21, he prayed for her to conceive and she did — twins! In Nehemiah 1:4, Nehemiah hears about the state of Jerusalem, he fasts and prays. God answers exceedingly!

God is a trustworthy God who answers prayers. The answers don't always come when we want them; sometimes it feels like He will never answer. But God hears and responds to every prayer prayed to Him. There are times in the Psalms where David, a man after God's own heart, cries out to God, over and over again, to hear his prayer (Psalm 86:6, 102:1).

There are so many things to pray about. Many of my prayers have to do with someone or something that might personally affect me. Yes, I pray for other things, but the things that are around me like sicknesses, trials, and needs, I have a tendency to go to God with these over and over again. These are usually the needs or prayer requests of my friends, family, co-workers, or neighbors. I see this same pattern of prayers by those who prayed in the Bible.

In Matthew 6, one of Jesus' disciples asked Him to teach them to pray. Jesus says, "When you pray, say: Our Father in heaven, hallowed be your name. Your kingdom come, your will be done, on earth as it is in heaven. Give us this day our daily bread, and forgive us our debts, as we also have forgiven our debtors. And lead us not into temptation, but deliver us from evil." This prayer has a lot to ask about what we need.

Prayer is the place you can take your burdens and the things you are thankful for. We go to God because He is our source of hope and encouragement. We must go to God by first blessing Him (hallowed be Your name). Then we also need to ask for His help in our time of need. Jesus also tells us in Matthew 6:8, "Do not be like them (the hypocrites), for your Father knows what you need before you ask him." So even when we go to God in prayer, He already knows what we will pray for.

Jesus teaches us how to pray and request the things *we* need from our Heavenly Father. He knows that the

Father is the only one capable of answering prayer. He desires to provide for you and give you wisdom for every situation.

Today, take time to focus on your husband. Note the things he does that are right in your eyes and then thank God for these things. Then, take the time to bring before your Heavenly Father the things he needs, desires, struggles with, and to thank Him for his abilities.

Finally, take your husband by the hand, and find a quiet place where you will not be interrupted, and pray with him.

1. Think of a biblical person who prayed and God answered their prayer. What was the prayer and answer?

____

____

____

____

____

2. Write down a recent prayer you prayed and how God answered it.

____

____

3. Is there a prayer you have been waiting a while for an answer? If so, what is it?

4. Read Psalm 86:1-10. Write all the ways that David asked the Lord to listen to his prayer.

5. What are some of the things you are personally praying for? Who are some of the people you are praying for right now?

6. Focusing only on your husband, write down the things you will pray about to your Heavenly Father for him.

7. Read Daniel 9:18. Rewrite this verse in your own words.

Your Prayer:

Heavenly Father,

I thank You for ________________. You created him and set him apart to be my husband. Father, You do all things well. Keep him in the forefront of my mind so I will continually pray for him and that Your will would be done in his life.

In Jesus' name, AMEN.

Say It Loud: 

______________, can I pray for you? I want you to hear me thank God for you. (Take him by his hand and pray).

E.F.T.W. (Encouragement from the Word):

> *"Therefore, confess your sins to one another and pray for one another, that you may be healed. The prayer of a righteous person has great power as it is working."* James 5:16

A Cheer to Remember:

Together we stand *(clap, clap)*,
Together we fall. *(clap)*
All for one *(clap, clap)*,
And one for all!

CHEERLEADER TIP:

A cheerleader doesn't just cheer,
she inspires.

DAY 24

Can I Hold Your Hand?

~

There are many ways men have creatively taken to make the initial step of declaring their "love" for us. Remember the "I-like-you-do-you-like-me-check-Yes-or-No" notes passed in the first grade? How many pick-up lines can you recall? "Do you have a band-aid? Cause I just scraped my knee falling for you."

When your husband got past the initial step of declaring his affection for you, one of the most common next steps was reaching over and holding your hand. When you didn't pull away as if his hand was a hot potato, loosen, or reject the grasp, he knew he was safe. This was your simple way of saying, "I really like you, too." There is comfort in holding the hand of the one you love.

There are several reasons for holding of hands. One is the clasping of your own two hands. When you clasp your hands together, one of the major reasons is to pray. You are positioning yourself to plea to God. The other is to hold the hand of those you love.

As a mom, when I am in a crowd with my children, I always make sure we hold the hands of the ones who may get lost. To the crowd, my holding of this child's hand says, "he belongs to me." To the child, my holding his hand says, "my mom is here with me." To me, my holding my child's hand means, "you are safe."

Holding your husband's hand is a non-sexual form of physical intimacy. It is one way of letting those who see you know that you belong together. When you enter a room holding hands, it says you are here together. So hold hands. It is connection and safety.

1. Can you recall the last occasion where you were holding someone else's hand? What was it?

____

____

____

2. Can you remember the first time your husband held your hand? Write down that memory.

____

3. What do you think is the purpose of holding hands?

4. Read Isaiah 41:13. In your own words, explain what this verse means to you.

5. When is the last time you held your husband's hand? What this out of habit or was it purposeful?

Your Prayer:

Heavenly Father,

Thank You for ____________________.
Give us special moments where we can declare our love for each other by taking the time to hold hands.

In Jesus' name, AMEN.

Say It Loud: 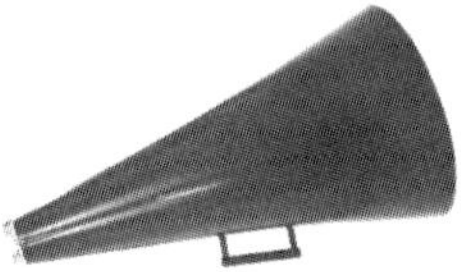

(Grab his hand)

________________, can I hold your hand? I want you to know I still like you.

E.F.T.W. (Encouragement from the Word):

> *"His hands are well formed, and he wears rings set with gems. His body is like smooth ivory, with sapphires set in it."* Song of Solomon 5:14

A Cheer to Remember:

Let me see you clap your hands!
What's that you say?
I said, let me hear you clap your hands!
(clap, clap, clap, clap, clap, clap, clap, clap, clap)
Now that you got the beat, let me see
you stomp your feet!
(stomp, stomp, stomp, stomp, stomp, stomp,
stomp, stomp, stomp)
I see that you're in the grove, so let me see your body
move!
(move your body, rolling it from top to bottom)

CHEERLEADER TIP:

Just as there is "no rest for the weary," there is no halftime rest for cheerleaders.

DAY 25

That Was Great the Way You Handled …

~

Women multi-task and are used to getting many things done at once. There have been many times where a situation arose and I immediately responded. If there is something that needs to be handled, I can handle it and go right back to whatever I was doing and never miss a beat. Sometimes, I can handle it at the *same* time. It amazes me when my husband is around that he doesn't respond too quickly to the same situation. I think, "How can he just sit there?"

As mothers and as women, we are wired in a way that we have to do something. If our children fall down, we are there in an instant to pick them up. When they are short on cash as they grow older, we search through our purses to give them what we have. But, I have seen Ray, as their father, wait. He has waited to see if the fallen child will get up, and if the child with money issues will find another way to make money.

There have been times when he deals with the situation and I have had to just smile as I think, "I would have *never* thought of that angle or taken that position." His forethought was brilliant and I am so impressed with his creativity. (I have also realized that many times my immediate response snuffs out *any* response from my husband.)

We need to encourage our men to handle situations in their own way and in their own time. Sometimes, our encouragement needs to be through silence. Some men process things at a different speed than women and we need to allow our husbands a chance to respond accordingly. Guaranteed they *will* handle the situation differently than we will. They probably will handle it like a "man" would.

There was one occasion when one of our sons did something he should not have done. I was ready to take matters into my own hands when my husband said he would handle it. Days went by, nothing had happened, and I was getting ready to step in and deal with the situation. But I waited.

Saturday rolled around and Ray called for this son to help with planting. We had a *lot* to plant, some things that required a man's ability to dig deep. I found out that day that this particular son was a lover of hard work and loved working in the yard. I would have never thought of this punishment because I didn't think a child this young could possibly do this adult work. My waiting on Ray left me not only impressed with my husband and son, but allowed me to see that I had underestimated both of them.

Our immediate and often emotional response has a place. We need to immediately respond when a child runs out into the street. We need to immediately respond when two children are physically fighting each other. But every situation is not life threatening. There is enlightenment in not handling everything, every time. As women, we need to wait, pray, and let our men respond like men.

In James 1:5, it says, "If any of you lacks wisdom, let him ask God, who gives generously to all without reproach, and it will be given him." God gives to women discernment; some call it intuition. We need to make certain we are responding to things out of the discernment that God gives us. This requires that we take time to ask God for His wisdom on most situations. This also requires that we wait on God to answer before we act.

When we respond, do we take the time to pray? Talk to God about the particular situation, and take the time to allow the Lord to tell us how to handle it. God is all wise and all knowing. And He desires to be a very present help in our time of need (Psalm 46:1).

Just as we need to allow God the time to answer us, we need to allow our husbands the time to respond to situations in our homes.

1. What was the circumstance of the last situation where you immediately responded and why?

____

____

____

____

____

____

a. Looking back on this, was it a life-threatening situation?

____

____

____

____

2. Write the circumstances of the last situation you allowed your husband time to respond to and how he handled it.

____

3. What are the differences between your response in question 1 and your husband's response in question 2?

____

4. Has there been a time where you did not immediately respond to a situation but stopped to ask God for wisdom before you acted?

____

a. Did you wait on God to respond?

5. Read again Psalm 46:1. Rewrite it here in the first person.

6. Read again James 1:5. Rewrite it here in the first person.

Your Prayer:

Heavenly Father,

__________________ handles things so differently than I do. Teach me to wait and trust him, knowing that the way I would handle things is not the right way, just a different way.

In Jesus' name, AMEN.

Say It Loud: 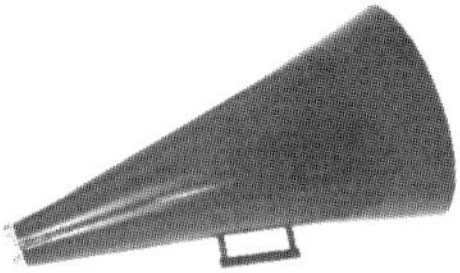

________________, that was great the way you handled (state the specific situation)! I would have never thought to handle it that way and I thank God for you.

E.F.T.W. (Encouragement from the Word):

> *"God is our refuge and strength, a very present help in trouble."* Psalm 46:1

A Cheer to Remember:

Dribble it!
Pass it!
We want a basket!

CHEERLEADER TIP:

She sets the pace of each game. She must keep smiling! She builds confidence and enthusiasm.

DAY 26

You Really Make Me Laugh

~

Laughter eases pain when all around you is somber.

At my grandma's funeral, everyone was sad. She was a godly woman, well-respected by all. At the repast, we began talking about the times she used to visit our home. She would make all of us, and any of our friends who were over, come inside at noon for prayer. She would have everyone bow on their knees and she would pray for a very long time. Many times we thought about crawling out but we were afraid of getting caught. As we sat around that table, reminiscing about grandma, we laughed so hard we cried.

Laughter can stop weeping and change the reason for your tears. Laughter is indeed medicine that is free and aids in curing whatever ails you.

During the Great Depression, money was scarce but people wanted and needed to be entertained. Shirley Temple movies were very popular for those who could afford to go; others listened on the radio to "Little Orphan Annie" as she and her dog solved mysteries. Outdoor games brought laughter and these times lessened the stress of the Depression.

Laughter is contagious and will spread to everyone in sight. Laughter is a funny face, an inside joke, or a tickle to just the right spot.

We all need some laughter and we need it often. Laughter needs to be at the heart of every home. The energy and ointment behind a healthy marriage is connected to both spouses' ability to laugh in spite of troubles.

Endorphins are hormones in your body that fight stress. One way to release these stress-causing agents is to laugh. It has to be genuine laughter and cannot be faked or put on.

What makes your husband hold his stomach, roll up in a ball, and laugh? Laughter is one component that will make life livable, and gives you the energy to go on. Laughter says, "Everything is going to be okay."

Your husband needs you to laugh with him — a lot. Laughter in your marriage will help him bear the load of his responsibilities. Your lives will never be easy because you have an enemy who is committed to making sure of that. But laughter is a load lifter. It will make whatever you bear in your family, in your life, or your commitments seem lighter.

Lighten your husband's load with laughter because where there is no joy, depression abounds. You can lighten his load by bringing joy and laughter to him in various ways. We sometimes need the simplicity of a funny movie. Laughter can also come by recalling a funny time, gesture, or moment that brought you to tears of joy.

Laughter will keep you youthful. Forgetting to laugh will cause you to become too serious about everything.

When is the last time you and your husband laughed together? Make it happen today.

1. Can you recall a time when a mood was somber and laughter changed the entire mood? Write down the details of this occasion.

2. Think of a difficult time in your life. What are some of the things you did (or others around you) to help you through this time?

____

____

____

____

3. Write down a time when you laughed because others were laughing. What made you laugh? (Facial gestures, laughter so hard someone has fallen to the floor, laughter where someone cuts the cheese, etc.)

____

____

____

4. Write a time where everyone in your home was laughing?

____

____

____

5. Read Proverbs 15:13. What does a "glad heart" (joyful, merry, cheerful) in this verse mean and what does it do to your countenance (face)?

____

a. Explain the last part of Proverbs 15:13.

6. When and what was the last laughter you and your husband shared?

Your Prayer:

Heavenly Father,

Teach me to never forget to laugh. Help me to be a catalyst of genuine laughter for ______________________________. Show me how to be a helper in lightening our load.

In Jesus' name, AMEN.

Say It Loud: 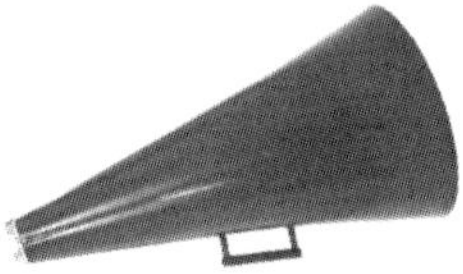

_______________, you make me laugh! I want to be able to laugh with you often.

E.F.T.W. (Encouragement from the Word):

> *"Whoever brings a fool into the world does so to his grief, and the father of a fool has no joy. A cheerful heart brings good healing, but a crushed spirit dries up the bones."* Proverbs 17:21-22 (NET)

A Cheer to Remember:

First and ten!
Do it again!
Come on team!
We're going to WIN!

CHEERLEADER TIP:

The refs are said to sometimes be blind. It's her job to make them deaf!

DAY 27

I Will Submit to Your Leadership

~

Most words beginning with S-U-B don't stand a chance of being a favored word or used frequently. Sub is a prefix of Latin origin meaning *under*. Sub means beneath or secondary to something that is before or primary. For example, substitute (only used when the primary teacher is not in), sub cranial (under the skull, covered normally by hair), submarine (a ship that usually runs under water).

When we hear the word *submission*, it is not very popular in any culture. But submission is a word near to the heart of God. This is the desire of God for His children; to submit (James 4:7).

God wants to lead His children to righteousness. He wants the world to see a true picture of His love for them. We are His ambassadors (2 Corinthians 5:20). He wants to make His appeal to the world through us. Our submission to His leadership displays a true picture of Christ's love for the church.

Some synonyms of submission are acquiescence, resignation, deference, surrender, and humility. Your Heavenly Father is asking you to continually show humility to Him by submitting to the leadership of your own husband.

God is a God of order and He orders the steps of those who love Him (Psalm 37:23). For there to be order in any organization or business, or in any church or home, there has to be someone who is in charge. Someone has to be accountable for the company, home, business, or church. Everyone else has to submit to that leader.

Your submission to your husband is you trusting God's order. God doesn't always let His followers know where He is leading them. When Abram was called to leave his family in Genesis 12:1, he had no idea where he would end up. God just asked him to follow and Abram followed by faith. Abram had bumps in the road, some he caused by his fear and his lying (Gen.

12:11-13), some heaped upon him by his own flesh and blood (Gen. 13:5-8).

Your submission to your husband doesn't mean you need to know the plan and once you know that he is on the right path, you will follow. Submitting to your husband doesn't mean things will go smoothly because you are following. But as you continue to trust God and submit to His appointed authorities in your life, you will grow in your faith.

Submission to your husband is you following on a journey with a plan known only by God. Following your husband's leadership displays your faith in God.

1. Write down one synonym for the prefix *sub* and explain why it may seem negative.

____

____

____

____

2. Why do you think submission is near to the heart of God?

____

____

____

____

3. What does humility mean to you?

____

____

____

____

4. How do you show submission to others leaders in your life?

____

____

____

____

5. What is the difference between a *projection* and a *sure thing*?

____

____

____

____

6. A leader of a corporation will have a projection for where the company will be next year. We have a sure thing in following Christ through the leadership of our husbands. Do you normally follow a projection or a sure thing? Why?

____

7. Read Genesis 12. Abram followed God, though not perfectly, and God richly blessed him. List some ways your husband has followed God.

8. How can your submission to your husband be a testimony of submission to God?

Your Prayer:

Heavenly Father,

I am afraid of what submission to ______________ may look like. I trust You completely and I know You will never leave me nor forsake me. I submit to You.

In Jesus' name, AMEN.

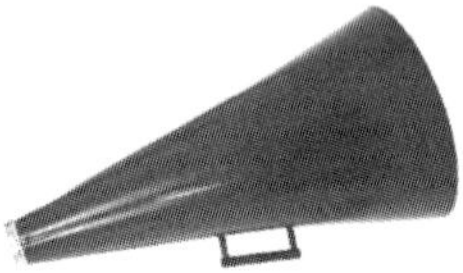

Say It Loud:

________________, I will submit to your leadership! God's ways are not always clear, but I will submit to you to bring honor to God.

E.F.T.W. (Encouragement from the Word):

> *"Likewise, wives, be subject to your own husbands, so that even if some do not obey the word, they may be won without a word by the conduct of their wives — when they see your respectful and pure conduct."* 1 Peter 3:1-2

A Cheer to Remember:

Push 'em back! Push 'em back!
Waaaaaaaaaaaaay back!

(repeat)

CHEERLEADER TIP:

She may not play for points in the game but she definitely changes the score.

DAY 28

I Will Never Leave You

~

On our wedding day, we said or repeated a lot of words. We made a lot of commitments ending these promises with seven small words, "as long as we both shall live." What we were saying is, "I will do all this because I will never leave you."

Every Christian marriage has an enemy. Satan is the foe of God and when you make a covenant to do marriage God's way, the enemy stages a devious plan to try to get you to regret and despise your pledge. Knowing it was never your intention to physically leave your husband, he set in motion a plan for you to "leave" without ever moving out.

Christian marriages have couples who have stayed together physically but have checked-out emotionally, spiritually, and sexually. In turn, we must set up guards to watch over each of these areas in our marriages. We must stay connected to our Father in Heaven and remain sensitive to His leading and His voice.

To stay emotionally connected in marriage, it takes extremely hard work and daily commitment. You must care and concern yourself with even the little things about your spouse (how's he doing, his job, his feelings, his loves and hates). We need to make sure to allow him time to unwind and open up. We cannot be okay with him responding to our questions about his day with "fine." It may take time to get him to answer your questions, as he learns to let you in.

To stay spiritually connected, we must be concerned about the godliness of our spouses. Praying for your spouse is the best way to care for him spiritually. Spiritual connection begins with your vested diligence to pray fervently for your husband. You need to take the time to ask him about the biblical things you have heard. What is his response or take on it? Spiritual connection means desiring to see your husband grow in his personal relationship with Christ.

To stay sexually connected, we must be willing to be sacrificial and deny ourselves sleep, T.V., or all the other things we think our homes and jobs require. We must be available and even schedule intimacy with our husbands if necessary. Because our lives are busy, we neglect physical intimacy to get much-needed rest. The opposite is true. When our spiritual, emotional, and sexual connection with our spouse is prioritized, our sleep is restful.

To neglect any area of your marriage (because expending the energy it would take to keep it fresh would be overwhelming) is *leaving*. It is abandoning this particular part of marriage because it requires more than you are willing to give. Things that are easy to us normally don't require much from us. Keeping from forsaking any area of your marriage may require much more than you think possible but with God, all things are possible (Matthew 19:26).

Promising, at our wedding, to never leave meant we will be available. Remaining physically in a marriage is easy as long as you have an easy marriage. Cleaving to your spouse requires going beyond easy. It is choosing to remain connected in areas that may require lots of energy and lots of prayer. If you have stayed in the marriage but have checked out of relating, it is time for you to completely come home and never leave again!

1. Which wedding vows have been easy for you to keep?

____

____

2. What are some ways you see the enemy attacking your Christian marriage?

3. If you had to name one area of your marriage where you have either checked out or feel like checking out, what would it be? Why?

4. Which area do you feel your spouse would have a tendency to check out or has already checked out?

5. Read Genesis 2:24-25. Give your definition of the word used in your version for "hold fast, be joined, unite, cleave, or embrace."

____

____

____

____

6. In your lifetime, list some things (outside of your marriage) that you have neglected. Write down the state of those things in your life now.

____

____

____

____

7. Whatever the state of certain areas of your marriage, what are some things you can do now to check back into (and renew) your relationship?

____

____

____

____

____

Your Prayer:

Heavenly Father,

I want a marriage that brings honor to You. I know there are areas in my marriage where I have checked out from ___________________. Teach me how to walk and listen to You, daily, hourly, and moment-by-moment. Guide me back to checking in.

In Jesus' name, AMEN.

Say It Loud: 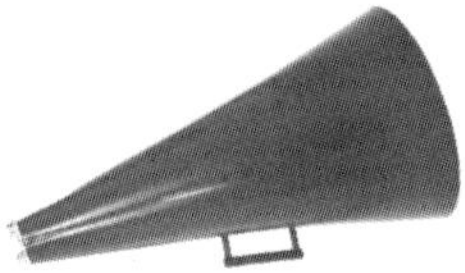

_______________, I will never leave you! I do not want to "check-out" from you in any area of our marriage.

E.F.T.W. (Encouragement from the Word):

> *"What therefore God has joined together, let not man separate."* Mark 10:9

A Cheer to Remember:

Don't gimme no bread!
(No bread!)
Don't gimme no meat!
(No meat!)
Just gimme that beat!
(What beat?)
That winning beat!

CHEERLEADER TIP:

She continually reminds her team that it doesn't matter whether they win or lose; it really matters how they play the game.

DAY 29

I See Christ in You

~

I know I am probably in the minority when I say I love my mother-in-law. She is witty, fun, humorous, and she is always dressed to the nines. But, this fun-loving lady will tell anyone when they have crossed a certain line. I am sure this five-foot-one-inch single mom had to assert her authority, verbally, in her home many times to be listened to.

My husband has taken on many of his mom's traits. As he grew up living with her, she unknowingly passed on many things that he has adopted. He is witty, fun, humorous, and cares about how he looks when he leaves our home. Even though they are two separate individuals, I see Ray's mom reflected in him almost every day.

I also see other glowing traits in my husband that stem from his spending time with God. I see the care, compassion, love, encouragement, and mercy of Christ in him. But, sometimes, I see the tough love, him pushing me to good works, how he builds me up to be more like Christ, and telling me to check my attitude when it stinks.

Sometimes I don't want to hear it because Ray isn't God. Exactly! Ray isn't God. I must admit, though, that he often acts, talks, and responds like Him because he desires to be obedient to Him and he spends time with Him.

Your husband is not God and will never represent Him perfectly. But, if your husband is a believer in Christ, you will see glimpses of Christ in him as you journey through this life with him.

In 1 Corinthians 11:1, Paul says, "Be imitators of me, as I am of Christ." It is time for us to look at our husbands and notice the resemblance of Christ in them. I can see that my husband looks a lot like his mom. I see the curly waves in his hair from his grandfather. But I also see a stark resemblance to His Father in Heaven whom he has followed since the age of fifteen.

1. Specify some traits or looks that your husband received from his parents.

____
____
____
____
____

2. List some ways (looks, personality) that you are like your parents.

____
____
____
____
____

3. What are some of the things your husband does because of his relationship with the Lord? (Reads his Bible, prays, teaches Bible studies/classes, etc.)

____
____
____
____
____
____

4. What are some specific godly qualities you see in your husband?

5. Take time and pray for your husband right now. Ask God to grow your husband to be more like Him. (If he doesn't know Christ, pray for his salvation.)

6. Read 1 Corinthians 11:1 again. What are some qualities you would like your family to see in you as you imitate Christ?

Your Prayer:

Heavenly Father,

I want to see more of Christ in ____________________. I pray he becomes an example of Christ to all he comes in contact with and every place he goes. Help me remember to pray for his continued growth in You.

In Jesus' name, AMEN.

Say It Loud: 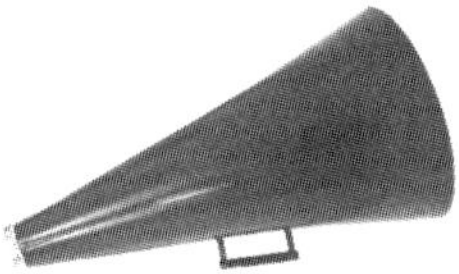

________________, I want you to know I see Christ in you.

E.F.T.W. (Encouragement from the Word):

> *"And you became imitators of us and of the Lord, for you received the word in much affliction, with the joy of the Holy Spirit, so that you became an example to all the believers in Macedonia and in Achaia."*
> 1 Thessalonians 1:6-7

A Cheer to Remember:

Let's get a little bit louder, saying,
LET'S GET A LITTLE BIT LOUDER!

(repeat)

CHEERLEADER TIP:

A cheerleader without cheer is like soda without the bubbles. Flat!

DAY 30

I Know God Made Me Just for You

~

After God created the world, vegetation, animals, land, and sea, God created man. God called man Adam. As God looked on Adam, He said it was "not good" for this man to be alone. So God created a helper fit for him. That helper was Eve (Genesis 2:18-23).

Eve was Adam's perfect fit. She was created to fill the lonely void that Adam had. God created all that Adam would need. He had food from the trees and vegetation. He had water to drink. He had sun to light his day and the moon to light his nights. Adam had all he needed but companionship. But God took care of even that need by creating Eve. Eve completed Adam.

Even before your husband was being formed in his mother's womb, God had a plan and purpose for his life. While he is fulfilling that purpose, God has created for him a perfect fit for him. A completer. You are God's creation for your husband. A helper fit for him.

Have you ever longed to have the gifts, talents, abilities, or looks of another person? Our human nature sometimes makes us desire things that we don't have, forgetting to notice all that we do have. We have all the elements necessary to fulfill the void of companionship our husband needs to accomplish his divinely given purpose in this life.

We need to see ourselves through God's eyes — why He created us with what we have, no more and no less. What is our purpose for living here, now, for this time?

God knows our unique strengths and weaknesses. He chose to create us with strengths where we need to be strong and weaknesses where we need to be weak. God knew we needed both. He didn't want us to only have strengths so we would forget to call on Him. He knew we needed weaknesses, too, so we would always depend on Him.

God knows we are the exact perfect person needed to sure up the weaknesses and encourage the strengths in our husbands. He created our husbands to be the exact match for us.

When God created Eve and brought her to Adam, he knew she was made for him. Adam said in Genesis 2:23, "This at last is bone of my bones and flesh of my flesh; she shall be called Woman, because she was taken out of Man."

Had God told Adam that Eve was taken out of him? Whether he knew or not, Adam trusted God and knew Eve was perfect for him.

Your husband is perfect for you and likewise, you are perfect for him. God has brought you together to erase loneliness in your lives. All that God creates is good.

1. What are some gifts, talents, abilities, or traits of yours that God has given you to help your husband? Why?

____
____
____
____
____
____
____

2. Why do you think God created you? What do you think is God's purpose for your creation?

3. Looking at why you are created and your purpose, what strength(s) do you have that your husband needs?

4. What weaknesses do you have that benefit your husband?

5. List some "good" things about you and your husband together that would not exist if you were apart.

6. Read Genesis 2:24-25. Rewrite these verses in your own words.

Your Prayer:

Heavenly Father,

You created me just for ___________.
As I walk with You, give me the wisdom and grace to fulfill the task You created for me. I want to stand before You a "Good and Faithful" servant.

In Jesus' name, AMEN.

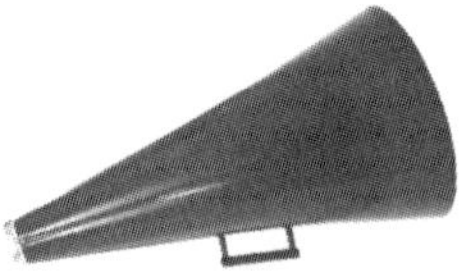

Say It Loud:

_______________, I know God made me just for you! I am his perfect fit for you and I will make sure I fulfill my created purpose.

E.F.T.W. (Encouragement from the Word):

> *"For we are his workmanship, created in Christ Jesus for good works, which God prepared beforehand, that we should walk in them."* Ephesians 2:10

A Cheer to Remember:

We've got that pride,
We've got that spirit.
So, come on fans, let's hear it,

So, wave your hands,
Scream out loud,
Come on, fans,
Shout, shout, SHOUT!

Write Your Own Story

Our God is so creative. No two things in His creation are exactly alike. So I am sure your husband is not exactly like mine.

You have a uniquely different, but special, husband. There is something specific that you can say to encourage him that no other husband in the world might need. You know what this specific encouragement is for him.

The following two "Write Your Own" encouragement pages are just for you to share and for him to read. He *needs* to hear these words from you and only you.

My prayer for us:

Heavenly Father,

I pray that You would give me the power and ability to become the cheerleader I desire to be. I want my words to give grace to all who hear them. Set a guard over my mouth when I feel the need to say anything that would not build my husband up. Keep watch over the door of my lips, for my desire is to build up and encourage. Thank You for creating me as a wife to be the encourager of my husband.

In Jesus' name, AMEN.

E.F.T.W. (Encouragement from the Word):

"And you were dead in the trespasses and sins in which you once walked, following the course of this world, following the prince of the power of the air, the spirit that

is now at work in the sons of disobedience-among whom we all once lived in the passions of our flesh, carrying out the desires of the body and the mind, and were by nature children of wrath, like the rest of mankind. But God, being rich in mercy, because of the great love with which he loved us, even when we were dead in our trespasses, made us alive together with Christ — by grace you have been saved — and raised us up with him and seated us with him in the heavenly places in Christ Jesus, so that in the coming ages he might show the immeasurable riches of his grace in kindness toward us in Christ Jesus. For by grace you have been saved through faith. And this is not your own doing; it is the gift of God, not a result of works, so that no one may boast. For we are his workmanship, created in Christ Jesus for good works, which God prepared beforehand, that we should walk in them." Ephesians 2:1-10

Write Your Own

Write Your Own

APPENDIX I

CHEERLEADER QUALIFICATIONS

Each and every cheerleader candidate must possess certain qualifications to encourage her team to victory:

1. A great cheerleader must maintain a positive attitude about her team.

> "Finally, brothers, whatever is true, whatever is honorable, whatever is just, whatever is pure, whatever is lovely, whatever is commendable, if there is any excellence, if there is anything worthy of praise, think about these things. What you have learned and received and heard and seen in me — practice these things, and the God of peace will be with you." (Philippians 4:8-9)

2. *A great cheerleader must be willing to fight for the good of the team.*

> "Live in harmony with one another. Do not be haughty, but associate with the lowly. Never be wise in your own sight." (Romans 12:16)

3. *A great cheerleader must maintain her mental, physical, and spiritual health.*

> "Or do you not know that your body is a temple of the Holy Spirit within you, whom you have from God? You are not your own, for you were bought with a price. So glorify God in your body." (1 Corinthians 6:19-20)

4. *A great cheerleader stays well-hydrated throughout the course of each game.*

> "...but whoever drinks of the water that I will give him will never be thirsty again. The water that I will give him will become in him a spring of water welling up to eternal life." (John 4:14)

5. *A great cheerleader rehearses her cheers by being well-versed in the "cheerleader's manual."*

> "Your word is a lamp to my feet and a light to my path." (Psalm 119:105)

6. *A great cheerleader must take inventory of other activities that may not be advantageous for her to be the best cheerleader for her team.*

> "All things are lawful," but not all things are helpful. "All things are lawful," but not all things build up. Let no one seek his own good, but the good of his neighbor. (1 Corinthians 10:23-24)

APPENDIX II

THE CHEERLEADER'S QUIZ

1. When your team is not faring well in the game and may be behind, do you:
   A) Encourage your team to QUIT.
   B) Encourage your team to FIGHT ON.
   C) Say nothing at all.

2. When your team seems to be in rut, do you:
   A) Think of creative ways to build up your team.
   B) Encourage your team to QUIT.
   C) Say more discouraging words to them.

3. When your team is not around you, do you:
   A) Continue to say positive things about your team.
   B) Put your team down with your words or actions.
   C) Say nothing at all about your team.

4. When you are tired and just don't feel like cheering, do you:

A) Not show up at the game.

B) Hand over your position as head cheerleader to someone else (your children, his co-workers, his mother).

C) Find strength (in prayer and God's Word) to rise above your feelings.

5. When your team gives you a valid reason for not wanting to cheer for them, do you:

A) Say more discouraging words to them.

B) Put your team down with your words or actions.

C) Encourage your team to QUIT.

D) None of the above; just be still and pray.

6. When the enemy of your team continues to plague you with doubt about your team, do you:

A) Agree with the enemy and give up.

B) Drown out his voice with LOUDER praise.

C) Find your strength in your weakness through Christ because you can do all things through HIM.

D) B and C above.

APPENDIX III

STEPS FOR CHEERING FOR A "LOSING" TEAM

(Read the truth of the bolded print!)

1. Realize every team has the potential to wipe out its enemy, so the enemy comes at these teams with all he's got.

> "The thief comes only to steal and kill and destroy. **I came that they may have life and have it abundantly**." (John 10:10)

2. Understand that everyone will have a period where things are not perfect. Make lemonade from the lemons that may be on your plate right now. Then share your lemonade!

> "Older women likewise are to be reverent in behavior, not slanderers or slaves to

> much wine. They are to **teach what is good**, and so train the young women to love their husbands ..." (Titus 2:3-4)

3. It seems as though you have always had a losing team and you want to give up; you are afraid to trust your current team.

> "...for **God gave us a spirit** not of fear but **of power and love and self-control**." (1 Timothy 1:7)

4. You are at a place where you despise your team. You can't even stand being on the same field with them. You feel you must quit in order to have sanity.

> "...Pursue righteousness, godliness, faith, love, steadfastness, gentleness. **Fight the good fight of the faith. Take hold of the eternal life to which you were called** and about which you made the good confession in the presence of many witnesses." (1 Timothy 6:11b-12)

5. Your team seems to have no fight left in them. It is the team *everyone* expects to lose and you don't have much hope for your team, either.

> "But **God chose** what is foolish in the world to shame the wise; God chose what is weak in the world to shame the strong; God chose what is low and despised in the world, even things that are not, **to bring to nothing things that are**, so that no human being might boast in the presence of God. And because of him you are in Christ Jesus, who became to us wisdom from God, righteousness and sanctification and redemption, so that, as it is written, "**Let the one who boasts, boast in the Lord.**" (1 Corinthians 1:27-31)

6. Finally, you must KNOW that there are no losers when God is the Captain of your team!

> "But thanks be to God, who gives us the victory through our Lord Jesus Christ. Therefore, my beloved brothers, be steadfast, immovable, always abounding in the work of the Lord, knowing that in the Lord your labor is not in vain." (1 Corinthians 15:57-58)

www.robynmckelvy.com